W9-AUE-056

WHITE FLAG

JUDY L. MANDEL

LEGACY BOOK PRESS LLC
CAMANCHE, IOWA

advance praise for
WHITE FLAG

"We rarely know the deeper ramifications of tragedy through people's lives. Judy L. Mandel's book *White Flag* shows us the true story of how the same tragedy I drew from for *In the Unlikely Event* spiraled through her family, giving a glimpse of the way trauma can be felt for generations."

–Judy Blume

"Judy Mandel's new memoir, *White Flag*, is both harrowing and heartbreaking. It's also strangely timely. Though deeply personal and intimate, the book asks us all to consider our own agency - and lack thereof - when things go terribly wrong."

–Richard Russo, Pulitzer Prize-winning fiction writer, author of nine novels, his most recent being *Chances Are . . .*, as well as short fiction and essay collections and screenplays.

"Judy Mandel's second memoir, *White Flag*, plumbs the depths of the original generational trauma that affected not only Judy's parents, but their children and grandchildren. While the book focuses primarily on Judy's own journey in trying to help her drug-addicted homeless niece, it also explores the larger issue of how psychiatric help is practically non-existent for the constantly growing number of homeless people in the United States. Quotes from recent studies of trauma-related addiction greatly enlarges the scope of the memoir, as does Judy's own personal journey through the red tape associated with navigating the bureaucracy. I have not read a memoir that so carefully and personally explores the difficulties associated with trying to help an addict find the proper treatment, when insurmountable obstacles — including the addict's and the writer's own denial — bar the way to peace and recovery. An extremely important and timely book that is a lifeline thrown out into the cold and unforgiving ocean that is our present time."

–KAYLIE JONES, award-winning author of *A Soldier's Daughter Never Cries, Speak Now, Celeste Ascending, Lies My Mother Never Told Me, The Anger Meridian.*

"*White Flag* is a unique blend of an emotional, scientific, psychological, and historical journey to understanding substance use disorder as Mandel seeks the reasons for her niece's addiction. There is solace in this understanding, and healing in seeing the limits of our own power over another—even those closest to us."

–MAUREEN CAVANAGH, author of *If You Love Me – a mother's journey through her daughter's opioid addiction*

"In her book, *White Flag*, Judy Mandel tells a most moving story of her niece's descent into drug addiction and the author's efforts to try to rescue her. This book opens our eyes and hearts: the suffering from trauma can be transmitted from one generation to the next. The author offers a loving testimony to her family's losses, to our human succumbing to suffering but also to our capacity for transcending tragedy by remembering and ultimately by surrendering ourselves to the life source."

–Kristina Schellinski, M.A., Psychoanalyst and Teaching Supervisor with the C.G. Jung Institute Zürich, Küsnacht, and International School of Analytical Psychology, Zürich, Switzerland. She is the author of *Individuation for Adult Replacement Children: Ways of Coming into Being.*

For Cheryl

contents

PART *ONE*

LOST IN THE RAIN

JUNE 15, 2014

I AM CERTAIN THE PHOTO ON MY COMPUTER SCREEN is Cheryl, my sister Linda's daughter. In some ways she looks the same. Her mother's eyes, her father's full round face, her thick hair like mine. But her eyes are empty, unfamiliar. What do I expect from a police mug shot? The important thing, I tell myself, is that I've found her. Even if she doesn't know she's been found, surely she knows she's lost.

My sister's birthdate popped up in my Google calendar this morning, though she's been dead for five years, and I felt compelled to look again for Cheryl. I almost wrote, *Linda made me look.*

What exactly am I trying to do? Locate a better future? Heal the past? Or am I just trying to keep my last promise to my sister to keep her daughters safe? When I type in Cheryl's name, I have three other windows open: Facebook, a travel site, and a search for Hillary Clinton's new book. It occurs to me that these threads of my online life—where I search, with whom I engage— form a kind of fabric of my unfolding story. On this warm June day, I stare out my window to watch neighbors walking dogs and babies in strollers.

For the last two years I've imagined Cheryl living on the streets—or dead. Shocking though this mugshot from an Ohio jail may be, I'm terribly relieved. Also overwhelmed by how much I love her. Whatever trouble she is in, she is still mine.

Cheryl has been lost, found, and re-lost many times. When she was using, she removed herself from the family. Once, when I found her in a motel, her mother frantic to find her, she yelled, "I don't want you to see me like this," and slammed the door in my face. At times she returned to our lives, only to disappear suddenly, usually taking money or jewelry. Understandably, many people judge addicts as unworthy of our help.

Remembering how Cheryl helped her mother and grandparents when they needed her, how she doted on a collection of dogs and cats, I hold on to my belief that she is compassionate and caring at her core. She's funny and open and loving—the girl I miss.

Now, Cheryl's dark eyes stare at me from my computer, calling me to take some kind of action. Because there is no one else. Her mother is dead, her father has mostly given up on her, and her younger sister, Debbie, has her own problems right now. For a long while, I was afraid to find her. I tend to look away from things I don't want to see.

The caption under her photo posts the date she was incarcerated, her age at 40, and the charges:

Possession of a controlled substance (heroin); false identification; escape; loitering with intent of prostitution.

A vision of Cheryl at age seven in pigtails, wearing her red jumper is suddenly in my head.

I slap my laptop shut.

When I re-open it, she's still there, pleading.

I address an email to the Ohio prison.

SUBJECT: Inmate #1532234.

LETTER FROM CHERYL

June 2014

Sorry it's taken me so long. I only get 2 envelops a month.

Being indigent. No one on the outside to help me.

We get a bar of soap, small toothpaste. I trade my envelopes for hygiene stuff.

I go without soap often.

Sorry you haven't been well. Sorry I wasn't there. I pray for you every night.

Hope you are better.

I'm well, just struggling, in a place called Talbert House for alcohol and drug addiction affiliated with the jail.

Send me a copy of your book. Some of the girls want to read it.

Can you send Debbie my address here?

Doing the best I can.

Love always,

Cheryl

LEAN ON ME

THE ENVELOPE IS CREASED DOWN THE MIDDLE and the return address is just Cheryl's name and inmate number. It's been three weeks since I wrote to her, and I had nearly given up on hearing back. Her letter is written on both sides of a white, wide ruled piece of paper that looks like it was ripped from a notebook. The printing, in pencil is large and thick. I situate myself in a comfortable chair in my living room to read it. No one is home except me and my cat, Simon. He crawls up beside me and pushes his head under my palm.

Being indigent. No one on the outside to help me. I shake off this obvious attempt to engender my sympathy. There is no denying that she needs me. Though I have let her father and her sister know where she is, I haven't had any indication from them that they will be in contact with her or lend any support.

Why had I resisted finding her? Was I afraid she was in such deep trouble that my meager lifeline couldn't reach her? In prison, I tell myself, at least she is safe, and I hope she isn't getting any of the drugs that put her there. If not enough soap is the only problem, I can solve that. Of course, I'm worried about everything I've read about women in prison: the abuse by guards, the easy access to drugs, the violence. Watching too many episodes of *Orange is the New Black* doesn't help. But you can only worry about so many things at one time.

Strangely, Cheryl's letter further muddles my vision of her living conditions. Is this a house she's in? Part of the prison— but not? Does she have a room and a private bath? My imaginings have been along the lines of what I'd seen in movies and TV. A small bunk, shared showers, burly women demanding her M&M's or else. Is this a kinder and gentler incarceration?

The fact that she's in a rehab program is encouraging. She'd been through many, starting when she was a teenager. Hopefully this one will help her understand how to quell the demons that drive her to self-medicate. What I believe she's done her whole life. I fight the idea that there is a time limit on fixing one's life.

Six or seven years ago we walked around my parents' Florida condo complex, tiny lizards scurrying into bushes and the sun branding my neck. She had a steady job then as an office manager and a live-in boyfriend who I thought was a good guy. I asked Cheryl what she was doing to stay on the right road.

"Are you going to meetings?"

"They aren't for me," she said. "I don't really need them. I just know I'll never go back to that. That part of my life is over."

She swept aside her long, black hair and looked steadily into my eyes. When she noticed my discomfort with her answer, she smiled and put an arm around me.

Why didn't I challenge her bravado then? Was I still trying to be the cool aunt? I remember being relieved that she answered me at all and was anxious to leave the topic alone.

I write back to Cheryl on my mother's birthday, July 7, addressing the letter to her grandma's nickname for her—Cher. I think of her by that name now. *Grandma loved you so very much*, I write. In my heart, I am happy my mother did not live to see her granddaughter in prison—which I do not say. I think another terrible thought; that my sister's death was also fortuitous, sparing her this added anguish.

I do my best in my return letter to prove to Cheryl she has someone on her side who loves her, and I applaud her reaching out to the rehab program. *You are stronger than you know.* These efforts have a fortune-cookie echo, but I'm using every tool at my disposal. Sometimes platitudes serve a purpose.

I ask her if she knows that depression runs in our family. Not only Grandma and her mother, but others in our extended family? Has anyone told her about the suspected suicides with coverups rivaling Watergate? Is her therapist helping her understand her addiction? Is she receiving any medication?

I write that I'm reading about the disease of addiction, hoping that designation may take away some of her guilt and shame and open up our communication. She is deserving of help and love, I repeat in as many ways as I can manage.

Mental health care, housing and employment are the basic essentials when she gets released, so I ask about any discharge planning at the prison.

After speaking to a colleague who is a social worker and has experience with the prison system, I understand it's important to put money in Cheryl's commissary account.

"They really need it to buy necessities," my friend tells me. "Also, it makes them feel like someone on the outside cares about them. She'll be able to buy things like hair conditioner, soap and toothpaste, and some luxuries like soda."

The system for depositing commissary money on the prison website is complicated, and I discover they charge you money to deposit money. It's the same for setting up an account to allow the inmate to call you. Both are administered by third parties, and I'm beginning to feel disheartened by the exploitation. But, as they are aware, I am at their mercy in trying to support my incarcerated loved one.

Her first phone call comes when I'm at the beach with my husband, celebrating our anniversary at a favorite Rhode Island hotel. We're having lunch at an outdoor restaurant when I answer the phone and am startled to hear the automated recording from the prison, stating her name and asking if I will accept the charges. I leave my lobster roll on the picnic bench, mouth "Cheryl" to David, and walk quickly to the edge of the parking lot where the signal is stronger. My heart is racing.

"I tried calling a few times, but there was no answer. This was the last time they let me call today," Cheryl says.

"The signal here is bad, I'm so sorry. I never heard it ring." I hesitate telling her I am at the beach. It seems cruel.

"Oh, no problem, I'm glad you picked up and I can hear your voice. I know you won't always be able to answer, so don't worry. Have a great time and ride a wave for me."

I flash on an image of her at ten in her first two-piece bathing suit and boogie board at the Jersey Shore.

Next week, I'm headed to a writing conference, I tell her, but we can still talk on the phone and write letters. Books are on the way too, sent through Amazon, as required. All books must come directly from third party suppliers, which I understand is for security, but still feels like more exploitation.

When we end the call, I sit on the rough wooden steps of the restaurant deck to compose myself, the sun hot on my back. A new tether to my niece is in place, feeling both familiar and foreign. It feels like I am suddenly immersed in a new world where I must find my way, like the first day of school or moving to a new city. It reminds me of my first trip abroad, getting off a train in Rome, feeling alien and lost. But the stakes for navigating this new environment are higher than finding a hostel and a meal. Cheryl's survival seems to rest with me, and I set my jaw and clench my fists.

BEGINNINGS

> The cruelty of children is immense, almost startling in its precision... Every whisper I heard was a comment about the way I looked, every laugh a joke at my expense. This singularity of meaning—I was my face, I was ugliness...
>
> — LUCY GREALY
> *Autobiography of a Face*

I WAS KEENLY AWARE OF what it meant to my sister Linda, Cheryl's mother, when she married. More than the high wire thrill of falling in love, she finally knew it was possible for a man to see through her scars, to see her, to love her. Her physical scars formed a cratered, tough red and brown landscape, descended from just under her cheekbones down her neck. The left side of her body was more burned than the right, wrapping tight, shiny scars around her upper arm down to the fingers. The burned left leg would give her more trouble later in life. These scars were the evidence, confronted every day of her life, that she had survived the explosive fire of a plane crashing into her living room when she was just two years old. That accident took the life of her older sister and lit another fuse deep inside the soul of our family. Her survival was deemed a miracle by the nuns and nurses at the Catholic hospital where she was first taken and where she stayed for the better part of a year. For the next 18 years, she had a surgery every year.

As her little sister, arriving on the scene two years after the defining accident, I witnessed the pain my sister endured throughout her childhood because of her scarred face—especially the face. Other scars and gnarled joints were covered by clothing. The deepest scars she hid with her smile. She once said, as she doused herself with perfume before going to a dance in high school, "Maybe if I smell good, they won't notice how I look."

Children were especially cruel when she was young. A scream of "What happened to her?" or just "Ewww" from little ones. My mother took the approach of quelling what she deemed normal curiosity, explaining, as simply as possible, about the plane crash and fire that left Linda scarred; leaving out the part about her seven-year-old, Donna, being killed. That was too much for children. As she got older, Linda took the same tact, telling a boy staring at her at the movies, "Turn around, you're missing the best part," or "Take a picture, it lasts longer." Later, adults parsed their cruelty more subtly. Refusing her jobs as a speech therapist, which she had trained to be, "because you might scare the children," or relegating her to the back office of a medical practice. I wish now I had helped her fight some of these injustices.

She never talked to me about her feelings of inadequacy and low self-esteem that I now believe she felt all her life. The evidence often manifested in her choices of men, or rather her acceptance of the deeply troubled men who chose her. Her first husband, Phil, was an anomaly. They'd met in college at a dance, married after graduation and both pursued careers: his as a chemical engineer, hers as a speech therapist. Did Linda's feeling of unworthiness also filter down to Cheryl? Would it have been different if Linda had dealt with the effects of her trauma with therapy as a child? Throughout her life, hiding her pain was as much to preserve my mother's facade of normalcy as it was to protect me. She wanted her little sister to be free of her baggage, taking a silent cue from my parents. We sailed along on the crest of that silence.

In *Autobiography of a Face*, Lucy Grealy describes the rare moments when she can forget her disfigured face:

Yet occasionally, just as that vast ocean threatened to swallow me whole, some greater force would lift me out and enable me to walk among them easily and carelessly, as alien as the pony that trotted beside me, his tail held high in excitement, his nostrils wide in anticipation of a brief encounter with a world beyond his comprehension.

My sister had these moments too, when she walked in her life unfettered. Her wedding day to Phil was one such day. The joy nearly burst through the roof at the elaborate celebration my parents hosted. The food never-ending and the dancing so raucous I thought someone would break a leg during the Hora. Family and friends were so happy to see Linda enter a happier phase of her difficult life. Older relatives remembered her as the charred baby girl carried from the flames.

Linda wanted children, but she wasn't sure it was possible after her many years of X-rays, anesthesia, surgery and medications. My parents whispered to each other that the radiation alone may have left her unable to conceive. That dark cloud dispersed when she became pregnant with Cheryl.

During the pregnancy, Linda and Phil went to Lamaze classes to learn how to breathe through the contractions, but when she showed me the whoo-whoo breathing technique, we collapsed into giggles, and she confided that she knew enough about pain not to count on any fancy breathing.

"I'm getting the epidural block," she said.

The pregnancy was deemed high risk, so my sister went to an obstetric specialist in New York City, traveling almost two hours from her home in Lakewood, New Jersey, for monthly appointments and then the birth. I remembered this later—that Cheryl's birthplace was New York City—when I needed to procure her birth certificate for health insurance.

I was nervous about Linda making the trip to the city in labor. It seemed dangerous. But no one consulted me. I was just the little sister, five years younger, who knew nothing about such things. Also, at the time, I was planning my own wedding. Linda was my Matron of Honor, so I fretted over her fitting into her dress after having the baby.

Whether the scar tissue around her torso could expand to accommodate the pregnancy was also a question. The taut burned skin of her abdomen had been spliced and grafted just after the accident to allow her to breathe. Gradually, as Linda grew pleasantly round, this worry dissipated. My mother, though, carried her basket of anxiety until the very day Cheryl was born and lay safely on my sister's breast.

When Cheryl was born, Linda seemed comfortable with

herself and settled into her life. She seemed happy in her marriage to Phil, and they had a second child, Debbie, less than two years later. But I know it is impossible to know what someone's marriage is like from the outside. My sister never explained the reasons for their divorce. Then came a stream of men who I felt took advantage of Linda, and frankly, failed to live up to the requirement of bringing in more money than they ate up—my definition of the absolute lowest bar when children are part of the equation. She always had a man in her life, sometimes in her house, and she married three more times. At the time of her death, Linda was divorced from her fourth husband.

My mother believed Cheryl's birth was a miracle—perhaps the reason Linda was the daughter spared when her older daughter was not. Trying to make sense of the senseless. And maybe why I need so desperately to help Cheryl now. Truly, it is like they are both looking over my shoulder.

LETTER TO CHERYL

JUNE 2014

Dear Cheryl,

Deposited $25 in your account. Buy some soap!

About depression. I read that the right meds can make all the difference.

You will make it! I hear your old self in your voice—which is wonderful!

I might sound like a cheerleader—ha!

Your mom taught me that we are stronger than we know.

Grandma used to say, "God only gives us as much as we can handle, and that which doesn't kill us makes us stronger."

Then she'd add: "I'm strong enough, God, so cut it out!"

Love,

Aunt Judy

CLUES

You see now that It's your enemy and your worst personal nightmare and the trouble It's gotten you into is undeniable and you still can't stop. Doing the Substance now is like attending Black Mass but you still can't stop, even though the Substance no longer gets you high. You are, as they say, Finished. You cannot get drunk and you cannot get sober; you cannot get high and you cannot get straight. You are behind bars; you are in a cage and can see only bars in every direction. You are in the kind of a hell of a mess that either ends lives or turns them around.

– DAVID FOSTER WALLACE

Infinite Jest

I AM STARKLY UNEDUCATED ABOUT ADDICTION, and hoping to help Cheryl, I commit to learn more. A friend recommends I read *In the Realm of Hungry Ghosts*[1], by Gabor Maté, a physician who treats addicts at the Downtown Eastside Vancouver clinic. The book is filled with case studies and scientific information about substance use disorder.

Maté begins with some history of the word addiction:

> *The term's original root comes from the Latin addicere, "assign to" (from dicere, "to say," and the prefix ad-, "to"). That yields the word's traditional, innocuous meaning; a habitual activity or interest, often with a positive purpose. . . But the Romans had another, more ominous usage that speaks to our present-day interpretation: an addictus was a person who, having defaulted on a debt, was assigned to his creditor as a slave—hence addiction's modern sense as enslavement to a habit.[2]*

The word enslavement conjures a picture of Cheryl in chains, rowing in the bow of a ship. Or maybe to be true to our Jewish roots, hauling mammoth stones to build the pyramids. The more I learn about Cheryl's experience, the more enslavement fits. No choice and no escape.

Maté goes on to talk about brain chemicals and nerve circuits, as well as psychological and sociological elements of addiction. But he warns: ". . . addiction is a complex condition, a complex interaction between human beings and their environment" [3] —a nuanced play between brain chemistry and social and economic forces. Reading Maté, I find myself trying to conjure the exact equation that led to so much suffering for

Cheryl.

Here are some of the facts Maté spells out that help me make sense of how addiction works. Serotonin and dopamine are brain chemicals that help us feel emotionally balanced. Dopamine is most associated with producing pleasure. Some people, the lucky ones, can get their dopamine hits from a walk on the beach or a kiss. Serotonin helps regulate moods and control impulses. Addicts often have lower levels of serotonin along with reduced dopamine pleasure receptors. This combination leads addicts to look for more intense dopamine triggers to achieve pleasure. It might be a certain drug, alcohol, eating, gambling, or sex. With less serotonin, they have less physical means of control. Tragically, flooding a brain with dopamine will further skew the chemical imbalance, so cravings increase. Because the brain is always learning, it learns this unhealthy pattern and comes to depend on it. Unfortunately, too, decision-making and the ability to self-regulate are further impaired by this imbalance, making the addict even more prone to stress, as Maté and others have substantiated through scientific studies and case-study observation.

The reason the War on Drugs doesn't work is that drugs are not the cause of addiction. Along with chemical imbalance, Maté asserts: "With my patients, the childhood trauma percentages would run close to one hundred."[4]

From his work with addicts, he contends that giving them access to drugs in a controlled environment reduces crime and allows for treatment and healing. This is what he does at his clinic. What this means with respect to our current opioid crisis, I'm not sure. I'm pretty sure the flood of opiates by big pharmaceutical companies has also fueled the epidemic.

What does all this mean in Cheryl's case? It seems to me that once addiction enters the equation, it becomes the central issue. The reasons behind what led to the addiction fade into the background as people just try to get clean and survive. What I want to know is what kept Cheryl doing something obviously detrimental to her well-being, making her do things she will forever be ashamed of—stealing from her mother and selling her body—and landing her in jail?

From Bessel Van der Kolk's book, *The Body Keeps the Score*[5], I learn more about brain function and how trauma and stress contribute to the propensity for addiction. The section of the brain called the amygdala works like a smoke alarm warning of a fire. It gets us ready to fight, run, or freeze. The medial prefrontal cortex then helps us assess the danger and the appropriate response. Is the house on fire or is the smoke coming from a steak burning on the stove? As a result of trauma, Van der Kolk explains, people with Post Traumatic Stress Disorder (PTSD) have difficulty processing information from their conscious brain—or medial prefrontal cortex—to determine whether outside stimuli is a threat or not. Everything seems to be a threat, and they tend to overreact to sounds, touch—anything out of the ordinary. They can be quick to anger. All of this contributes to additional stress and anxiety. Some may seek relief from this state of hyper anxiety with drugs or alcohol.

Where did this thread of trauma and post-traumatic stress begin for Cheryl?

Childhood trauma has been shown to have a tangible effect on brain development. A part of the brain called the vermis influences the dopamine system in the midbrain and is thought to play a key role in addiction. Scanned imaging of the vermis in adults who were sexually abused as children show abnormalities of blood flow, causing symptoms that increase the risk of substance addiction.[6]

In another study, the hippocampus (the memory and emotion center) was found to be 15 percent smaller than normal in depressed women who had been abused in childhood. The hippocampus remained unaffected in those who were depressed, but not abused.[7]

At this, I am thinking about the suspected abuse Cheryl may have suffered at the hands of her mother's second husband. I only heard whispers of it through the years. My sister never talked about it. Cheryl hasn't either. Why haven't I pressed her about this?

If abuse did occur, Cheryl's brain may have been almost pre-programmed for addiction. Not only might her brain development have been impaired by trauma, but when stress is added in childhood—real or imagined—hormones such as cortisol and adrenaline flood the body, including the brain's emotional centers, introducing even more risk for later substance abuse.

My quest to understand Cheryl's addiction is starting to feel like the old game of Clue, where you line up the suspects and figure out what weapon was used. I decide to use a white board in my office to begin tracking the possible culprits.

I list my first suspects:

BRAIN CHEMISTRY

CHILDHOOD ABUSE

LETTER FROM CHERYL

July 2014

Nice to get your letter. It means so much to hear from you, and to call and talk.

I understand you can't always answer, it's no big deal. I'll try here and there.

Working on discharge plan with my counselor, & housing plan and relapse triggers.

Depression is my big issue and I need to stay on meds.

Doxipan at night, Selexca *[sic]* in the morning.

I hope I find support when I get out. I know it's genetic,

I'll always have it.

LY

ESCAPE THE FIRE

Emotions are matter—real, physical, measurable matter in the form of our body's chemical makeup.

– KHALEGHI AND KHALEGH
The Anatomy of Addiction

H OW IRONIC THAT CHERYL IS FIRST DIAGNOSED with depression in prison. There is certainly some family history to consider. My mother, I know, suffered from nearly debilitating depression after the plane crash and death of her eldest daughter, Donna. I wrote a whole book, *Replacement Child*, about how my birth was meant to bring my mother out of that depression. Maybe it worked to an extent, but many times I would come home from school to find her in bed for no physical reason.

When the fire exploded from the plane crashing into their kitchen, my mother rushed her own mother and Donna's visiting friend, Sheila, out of the apartment. Sheila was on fire, and my mother wrapped a blanket around her to smother the flames before getting her out the door. She yelled for Donna to run but couldn't see her. Donna yelled back, "Get the baby, the baby is on fire!" Two-year-old Linda was engulfed in a ball of flame. Caught between her two daughters, my mother made her *Sophie's Choice* decision, rolling two-year-old Linda in a rug and down the stairs to the only outside door of the second-floor apartment. She heard the lock click, knowing it would keep anyone from retrieving Linda. She ran down the stairs to hand the smoking bundle to a man who had appeared at the door. The apartment's entire floor collapsed as my mother was held back from reentering the building to try to get Donna. She had no way of knowing then that Donna couldn't obey her command to run because she was pinned under a ceiling beam.

She told me, "I'll hear her voice calling, 'Mommy, help me!' for the rest of my life."

Cheryl's mother, my sister Linda, was the baby my mother rolled down the stairs. She had a life of trauma from the age of two when she nearly died in those flames. After her miraculous survival of third-degree burns over 80 percent of her body, her childhood was interrupted yearly with reconstructive surgeries. And now it occurs to me that mine was too when my mother disappeared to stay by her bedside in the hospital. By age 18, Linda had had around 100 operations. Fire had welded her chin to her chest, which had to be excised. Scar tissue tightened in healing and had to be released. Scorched skin was replaced with skin grafts. Only recently, with some of my own illness and surgery due to Crohn's Disease, have I come to realize the extent of PTSD my sister must have suffered. Before new drugs for anesthesia, for instance, the ether they used to put her to sleep made her violently ill for hours when she woke up from surgery. I am not sure how she faced a yearly operation for some 16 years until she called a stop to it with her Popeye declaration, "I am what I am." As the difficulties in her life wore her down, depression was her companion.

Once, she told me on the phone, "If it wasn't for my girls, I wouldn't stick around."

I might have said something inane in reply like, "Oh, don't talk like that." Looking back on that moment I realize I ignored her cry for help.

Of course, there is no way that Cheryl escaped that same feeling. Was her brain chemistry further skewed with her own trauma? An imbalance that led to anxiety and depression? She was sent to her first rehab facility in Colorado as a middle schooler, but there was the usual family silence about the details of this episode. Now, I still find it impossible to broach this history with her, a fist rising in my throat when I try.

What I do instead is look up the online criminal record of my sister's second husband, Cheryl's stepfather from the time she was five to seven-years-old, whom I'll call Mark. The first shocker is my sister is still listed under "Possible Relatives" for the husband she divorced at least thirty years ago. I'm tempted to call him, or go to the address listed, look him in the eye, and question him. Or kill him. Though he is much older now, I recognize his face in the photo—a mug shot. Of course it's a mug shot. The address in Florida is very near where my parents, my sister, and my nieces lived for decades. This fact, unknown to me until now, is quite chilling. Was Cheryl aware of how close he lived to her? Did he ever contact her? Why am I afraid to ask her?

His criminal record begins with his most current arrest in 2013. Domestic battery. And in 2012, Battery with Strangulation. Other charges include Retail Theft, traffic violations, Soliciting in a Roadway, DUI, Failure to Appear, Open Container. His record goes all the way back to charges as a minor for possession of alcohol. This digression into Mark's background fills in some of the missing threads, the darker colors in the tapestry.

Reading this account, it's getting difficult to rein in my own guilt, as the tentacles of abuse from this man surely reached my sister. Where the hell was I? Her sister, for godsakes.

Finding Mark's record lends credence to my suspicion of sexual abuse. He is a proven abuser of women. I want to be sure Cheryl gets the kind of treatment that will help her—though I am not sure that can happen in prison.

Dual-diagnosis treatment is being lauded currently as the gold standard for treating addicts, which means treating both the addiction itself and the underlying issue which led to the person turning to drugs.

I add bullets to my white board:

DEPRESSION

PTSD

DUAL-DIAGNOSIS

GOT TALENT

CHERYL AND I WOULD WATCH TV TALENT SHOWS together in our homes 1,000 miles apart and text each other about the acts. We did this for a while after her mother died. It started when she saw a singer/guitarist on *American Idol*. I got an unexpected text on my phone while I was watching the same show: "You should have been on a show like this! You are better!"

Years ago, I played guitar and sang in what we used to call Coffee Shops, and Cheryl loved my singing. It tickled me that she still thought of me this way, since I hadn't performed professionally for probably 30 years. She also asked me to send her some of my old songs, and I emailed her a few MP3s I'd recently recorded on my computer.

We judged the acts on *American Idol* and texted back and forth about which ones should win. She was more country; I was more rock 'n roll—but we appreciated any standout performer.

The singer we both liked best came in second on the show, but we followed her career for a while afterward, sending each other links to her new releases and concerts. We talked about meeting up at one.

When I look back at Cheryl's Facebook page, I can pinpoint the time in 2010 when she posted a video of the singer, Crystal Bowersox, singing *Farmer's Daughter*. Back then Cheryl watched those shows in the safety of her Florida home with her two cats and two dogs—one of which was her mom's little poodle named Peanut—and maybe her boyfriend sitting next to her. I imagine us both giggling at the texts, peppered with family jokes. Only a few years later, this scene seems like a mirage from another life.

If I could go back to one of those nights, I would call Cheryl to hear the timbre of her voice. To ask how she was dealing with her mother's death. To transform our virtual connection to real communication. I might have heard something in the way she spoke to alert me to impending trouble.

LETTER TO CHERYL

JULY 2014

Cher,

Your voice sounded good yesterday!

Congrats on getting your certificate for the program!

I found a workbook for Corrective Thinking that you mentioned and enclosed it here—which I hope they let through.

So glad you got the books.

Poisonwood Bible is one of my favs.

I forgot that the family photos in *Replacement Child*

are an added bonus for you.

Hope the books are a bit of an escape.

Love always,

Aunt Judy

DIFFERENTLY
THE SAME

LINDA MOVED TO FLORIDA to be closer to our parents when Cheryl and Debbie were eight and seven. She told me her husband, Mark, would be able to find more construction work in the warmer climate. They divorced not long after.

My own life was in turmoil at the time, my second marriage was not working, and I wondered what was wrong with me. I'd traded my first distant and withholding husband for a demanding, jealous, and abusive one. I was lonely in the first marriage, but this one exhausted me with nearly the opposite condition. A man who didn't trust me to work late at my newspaper job, and who once threw potatoes at me to get me off the phone. Cooked potatoes may have turned into a harmless mash-up, but these were raw and solid and hurt when they landed on an arm or thigh. Sometimes your body tells you what you deny with your mind, and this was what happened to me in this marriage. Within a year the anxiety and discord exacerbated my chronic Crohn's Disease until one day a flare up left me bleeding and weak; rushing home from work, hiding bloody clothes under my raincoat. By the time we split up, I believed it was to save my life. My friend spirited me away one night when my husband was out. Soon I found a small apartment, adopted a kitten, and stocked up on Stouffer's frozen dinners. I went to work and returned home each day, grateful for the calm.

When my whole mishpocha moved to Florida, I felt again as I had throughout my childhood—like an outsider in the family. Born after the defining event of the plane crash. Linda and my parents were in each other's lives daily. Cheryl and Debbie saw their grandparents nearly every other day. Almost like they were co-parenting with Linda. They never lived more than ten minutes or so from each other, and Linda relied heavily on them for help with her daughters after school and on weekends when she went out. Later when I had my own child, I was inwardly jealous of their closeness and wished my son had more family around. There is nothing quite like the loving gaze of a grandma or grandpa for a child.

When my mother complained about not seeing me more often, I reminded her, "You're the ones who moved a thousand miles away!"

Partly, though, I was afraid that living closer to them would suck me into their vortex, and my mother's voracious need. I was still that little kid pulling away from my mother's smothering hugs. And still feeling guilty for it.

Linda called me one New Year's Day, crying that her boyfriend, Dave, had taken the keys to her car and her house, leaving her stranded with her two girls. My protective impulse was immediate. Even though I was the younger sister, I'd looked out for Linda throughout our childhood. I'd stare down a kid who seemed on the verge of saying something hurtful to her about her scars, or asking her what disease made her look like that. Hearing the fear in her voice on the phone that day, I hopped a flight from Connecticut to her in Boynton Beach.

Cheryl and Debbie came running to me as I got out of my car, each tucking under an arm for a hug. They were always attached to each other back then, so close in age they were almost like twins. I followed them into the two-bedroom rental house. Linda emerged slowly from the bedroom, her makeup still on from the night before, the mascara smudged down her cheeks. I wondered why she hadn't taken off her makeup to sleep, and then realized the answer. She didn't want Dave to see her without makeup.

"I can't believe you came down here, I didn't think you would." She seemed to be in some kind of shock.

Glancing around the house, I recognized the clutter I associated with my big sister: half-filled coffee cups, full ashtrays, the kids' toys everywhere. Even as a child I had known I could never share a living space with Linda. As much as my mother tried to keep an orderly house, Linda was her foil, leaving a constant trail of towels and clothes. As an adult she became a chain smoker, and I could never stay long at her home. Walking into her house felt like being in my parents' bedroom when I was a kid, the only room in which my mother allowed my father to smoke his Winstons. The smell of smoke stayed in my clothes and hair until I could wash them.

Quickly, we discussed where Dave may have gone, how I could find him, and what she wanted me to do when I did.

"I just want my keys back."

He had in fact left the car but taken the car keys along with the house keys. I had the feeling the argument beforehand was the more dramatic part of the story—but she didn't offer details, and I didn't ask. Even as I dove into the situation, I managed to keep my distance, and I felt calm in knowing I'd return home after this mayhem was over.

We decided I should first take the kids to my parents' condo. Linda had not called them. She called me, a thousand miles away. But

I understood. She needed to keep up the façade of normalcy, that Dave was a good guy. This episode would destroy that fantasy in my parents' eyes. It told me, too, that Linda intended to keep him around.

"Jude, what are you going to tell them?"

I had no idea. "I'll think of something on the way."

Cheryl grabbed Debbie's hand and led her to my car. They seemed unfazed, joking and laughing during the 15-minute ride to their grandparents'. I turned up the radio and sang to them.

You could not hide anything from my mother. As soon as she answered the door and saw the kids in tow, her brow wrinkled, and she squinted at me.

"What's wrong? What has happened?" She didn't even seem particularly glad to see me.

"Linda's having a little issue, I'll explain later. Can the kids stay for a while?"

The girls had already zoomed into the apartment and smothered their grandfather in hugs. He was lifting Debbie onto his knee as I went out the door.

I found Dave at his usual beachside restaurant, as Linda had suspected. She told me he had been drinking for several days and to be careful. How, I didn't know. I'd met Dave one other time, so I recognized him sitting in a far corner, his too-big black rimmed glasses sliding down his nose and his face shadowed with a couple of days' growth. He smiled and waved me over, swept a strand of greasy black hair from his eyes. I dodged his move to hug me and sat opposite him.

"How've you been, Jude?" My sister's nickname for me.

"Don't call me that. Just give me Linda's keys."

"Have a coffee, visit a li'l, what's happenin' in Connecticut these days?" He poured what seemed to be half a canister of sugar into his coffee and stirred it absently.

I just stared at him.

"You know your sister is no angel, I can tell you." He aimed his dripping spoon at me like a knife.

"Don't talk to me about my sister. Just give me the keys."

I locked on his eyes and waited until he grudgingly dug in his pocket and forked over the keys.

Neither of the girls ever forgot that visit. Maybe it's one reason they looked to me as the family fixer.

I'd like to say Dave disappeared, but every few years he resurfaced. Even after Linda got married a third, then fourth time. There was something about Dave she needed—possibly she craved his need for her. I often thought he depended on her for his very survival. He was certainly a special brand of crazy. Dave had once told me, with my husband and son as witnesses, that he'd invented the "mobile restaurant."

"You mean a food truck?" my skeptical husband asked.

Dave told us how he'd discovered the waterbed and was the very first to sell them, and how he made a rock star of a local singer whom we later saw singing in the local dive. There was some nonsense too about using a prism to convert sugar into energy.

My sister may have felt unworthy of love, but she was a very loving person. She'd told me, "I can find something to love in just about anybody." In the depressed man she lived with for two years; in the younger blonde surfer who turned out to be illiterate; and in the man who swore he'd been abducted by aliens as a child.

I've thought a lot about why Linda and I both had multiple marriages and how our underlying issues were different. Where my father doted on my sister and assured her she deserved every good day she could find, he was reserved with his affection for me. He believed I didn't need his accolades.

As I overheard him tell my mother once, "Don't tell her how pretty she looks in the new dress, it will just go to her head."

Comparing me with my sister was not to be done, and I truly don't blame him. But I can't ignore how I tried to replace his love for a good part of my life.

There were many times I disagreed with the way my sister lived. I worried about the men Linda brought home while the girls were young. About her daughters' lax upbringing, so different from the way we were raised. When they were teenagers, their rooms were filled with overflowing ashtrays and food wrappers, with MTV blaring. I was appalled that Linda allowed them to smoke in their rooms. It seemed a chaotic childhood, with little in the way of rules, in sharp contrast to the proper behavior expected of us as kids. My parents were not extremely restrictive, but we knew where the lines were. The first time I said a curse word I knew my parents heard, after dropping a heavy book on my foot, I retreated in fear to my room for hours. No one ever mentioned it, and I now suspect they just collapsed in laughter. We were given a religious education and Bat Mitzvah, a moral foundation I pledged to give my boy. Linda chose not to give her daughters any religious education, and I believed it was a mistake. But I never said a word to her about it. I never felt I had a right to interfere with how she lived her life and mostly kept silent. Maybe I had absorbed my father's view that she gets a free pass after paying so dearly for survival. Whenever I found myself on the verge of criticizing her, I felt sick to my stomach. I feel that way even now, writing this.

Cheryl took an interest in Judaism as an adult and began asking me questions and reading about the religion. She considers herself Jewish, a link with her grandparents and our family lineage. Right now, this gives me hope.

LETTER FROM CHERYL

August 2014

I need to apologize for my handwriting.

They took my pens and I can only have a jail pencil.

Also, for my last letter, being so selfish and so needy and upset.

I had to laugh at myself for writing so upset and rashly.

Like I used to do with Mom for random problems.

Like when I had a flat and called Mom and she said, "What would you like me to do?"

LY,

Cheryl

SORRY

Guilt is one side of a nasty triangle; the other two are shame and stigma. This grim coalition combines to inculpate women themselves of the crimes committed against them.

— GERMAINE GREER

HER LETTERS ARE FILLED with apology after apology, for her lousy handwriting, for complaining about a bad day, for needing money in her commissary. She thanks me again and again for being there for her, for loving her. Cheryl does not believe she is worthy of my concern and attention. Of my love. Her feelings of shame and unworthiness are embedded in the ink. Sometimes I lift the paper to my face and breathe it in.

Her mother loved her unconditionally. Linda tracked her down, brought her to get help and believed in her time and again. She got her daughter back for a time, and I'm grateful there were several years before Linda died when Cheryl was again part of her life. Linda once told me, "She's the sensitive soul in the family, when she is well, we are very close."

Cheryl disappeared shortly after her mother died.

She left her Florida home, her two cats and two dogs in such a hurry that the animals were left in the house alone. Her boyfriend had just been arrested for growing marijuana in their spare room. Debbie later rescued the animals. The sisters had been on the outs for the last year. Debbie didn't want her two boys at Cheryl's house because she suspected the drug use and selling. It turned out she was right about that.

At the time, Cheryl drove to Ohio in a "borrowed" truck from work to an old boyfriend from middle school. Although she hadn't been in touch with him for twenty years, she claimed he was the love her life. She called me just once to tell me where she was.

"Be happy for me, Aunt Judy, I am in love." I wanted to believe her.

For a long time, the stigma and shame of having a family member who struggles with substance use stopped me from telling my friends about Cheryl. It was only when she was incarcerated that I began to tell friends who I thought might understand. Even then, I mentally screened people before confiding in them, trying to determine their balance of compassion and judgment.

The shame surrounding an addict is insidious. My sister kept many of the worst details from me. Now I wish we had talked more openly. In one conversation, when Cheryl had been missing for many months and I asked my sister how she was coping, she said, "I have to let go of feeling responsible, for my own mental health." She felt she had done everything she could and nothing helped. At the time, I remember thinking if it were my daughter, I would stop at nothing to save her. But I knew so little of what Linda had gone through trying to save her daughter. I knew so little of anything at all.

Guilt and shame permeate Cheryl's letters. For putting her family through the arrests, the disappearances, the fears for her life, the attempts at recovery.

Shame is like a virus among us.

OUR PRISON
VISIT

...when spring comes, it melts the snow one flake at a time, and maybe I just witnessed the first flake melting.

— KHALED HOSSEINI
The Kite Runner

I LEARN ON THE PRISON WEBSITE about video call visits—a kind of Skype, and schedule a virtual visit. We are both excited to see each other. Is Cheryl as nervous as I am?

Fifteen minutes before our first video chat, I perch my laptop on three big books so she isn't looking up my nose on the screen. My bookcase is my backdrop, and I check the view behind me to ensure nothing is amiss, although I have no idea what may be inappropriate in this situation. Books like *Naked Lunch? Junky? Lit?* I decide to leave Burroughs and Karr where they sit.

We have not seen each other in more than two years. I comb my hair and practice my smile in the mirror because I know my face is easy to read and I may look worried. My idea is to sculpt her vision of me. Positive Aunt Judy. Funny Aunt Judy. Competent Aunt Judy, who can still fix things. Maybe we both still believe this.

The system is not smooth linking up and I wonder why they don't just use Skype—which works much better. After a couple of misfires, static, and shut-offs, I see her on the screen.

Cheryl looks like herself. Why does this surprise me? Her hair is still long and black but shows three inches of gray roots. I feel tears welling up at my first sight of her. She smiles, but her eyes apologize for being in this place. Her loose prison garb, with wide horizontal black and white stripes, looks like a costume for convicts in an old movie. She sits at a round table in a large room, maybe a cafeteria. Other inmates are visible on their own calls, milling around, or passing by behind her.

A large woman with wild black hair wafts past and peers into the screen at me. I almost wave to her. Cheryl shoos her away with "Excuse me!" Cheryl gives me the same exasperated look she'd give her mom when asked to clean her room. Then she quickly laughs. The light in her eyes makes my chest ache and my eyes water again. It's a connection we have, being able to laugh together at life's absurdities.

When she exaggerates clearing the area behind her with a swipe of her hands, like an umpire calling a base run "safe!" we both crack up. I can hardly stop laughing, just like I used to with her mother. Irrationally, I am overwhelmed by the impulse to get her the hell out of there. My whole dead family seems to be hovering, imploring me, "Do something! Get her out! She is ours!"

After a few "how are you's", the conversation lags and I feel a mild panic. I don't want to waste our precious time together. I have so much I want to say, but I know I can't say it all now, and so I say none of it. I recognize the nausea that grips me, a paralysis stopping me from bringing up anything that might cause conflict during this short virtual visit.

I remember Cheryl loves animals.

"Want to see my cat?" I pick up my very fat orange cat who has been nuzzling my ankle and hold him up to the screen for as long as he will allow. "Meet Simon."

He squirms free and I drop him. That laugh again, lifting me. I flash on her two cats and two dogs she abandoned.

"Oh my God, he's so beautiful! But what the heck do you feed that kitty? He is huge!"

"Anything he wants." The old joke.

The harsh edges in her eyes have softened now and I'm so glad I thought of this. Maybe I should get a dog.

She thanks me again and again for helping her and being there for her. I'm grateful that she seems to be okay, even if it's only on the surface. Only at this one moment. I tell her that I've given Debbie the information about doing a video visit.

We talk for our allotted 15 minutes about how working in the kitchen is good work duty and makes the time pass quickly, and how much she likes the book I sent her, *The Kite Runner*.

Our call is finished, and I've managed to hold back my tears until the screen goes black. But I wish we had talked more about Khaled Hosseini's book, and the characters of Hassan and Amir; about how facing hard truths helps us to heal, but wounds left untreated will fester.

CHERYL'S FACEBOOK POST

Cheryl   •••
December 28, 2010 5:30PM

My Busa's getting spayed today. I'm gonna be a worried Mommy all day and night until I get my baby back tomorrow morning. Who's gonna drive me crazy tonight? I'll be lost without her 'til she's home safe again.

👍 Like   ↪ Share

LETTER TO CHERYL

AUGUST 2014

You don't have to apologize, that's what I'm here for. Vent away!

I hope you got *Sophie's Choice* I sent. When you read it you'll see why it makes me think of Grandma when the plane hit—deciding which child to go to in the fire. If she had gone to Donna, who was trapped under the ceiling beam, neither of us would be here.

Glad you are back at Talbert House. Glad they listened, when I told them how upset you were to be moved from there.

Sent $ to your account. Buy some underwear!

I can't get it out of my head that you wash one of two pairs in the shower each day.

Great job writing with the mini golf pencil!

Love,

AJ

THE BOXING RING

> . . . here was the secret of happiness, about which philosophers had disputed for so many ages, at once discovered: happiness might now be bought for a penny, and carried in the waistcoat pocket: portable ecstasies might be had corked up in a pint bottle: and peace of mind could be sent down in gallons by the mail coach, . . .
>
> — THOMAS DE QUINCEY
> *Confessions of an English Opium Eater*

THE LONG HISTORY OF OPIOID USE, beginning some 5,500 years ago, tells us that people have searched for centuries to escape their own reality.

Crack cocaine appeared on the streets of American cities around 1984. It was so called because it made a crackling sound as it was vaporized, due to impurities in the formula. This was, I believe, Cheryl's first drug of choice. She was using crack when I found her in a dingy motel in West Palm Beach.

She started using very young, an obstacle to recovery mentioned in many of the books I'm reading. How do I help her once she's out of jail? What do I do to keep her on the recovery path? Each book I pick up gives me a different approach and new methods. There is no one-size-fits-all treatment for addiction.

Some people can recover and stay clean totally on their own, or in outpatient programs, even without a 12-Step community program. But the 12 steps play an important role in recovery for many. Statistics show that those who go to Alcoholics Anonymous or Narcotics Anonymous, at least for a time, do better than those who do not. But Cheryl tells me, "It's not for me." Putting her fate in the hands of a higher power puts her off. It concerns me that Cheryl doesn't think she needs the help and may not even be aware of her underlying issues.

Medication for depression and access to mental health counseling will be crucial for Cheryl. I make a note to find out what will be available to her when she is released.

One book I'm reading advises not to pressure or judge. To listen and offer encouragement for good decisions as they come up; to offer options to solve issues. I try to do this in my calls and letters.

Relapse triggers can be anything associated with drug use—a street corner, a bar, a group of friends, a certain odor. It helps to make a behavior analysis, to list the kinds of substance abuse, when they are used and with whom, in order to understand more about triggers for relapse. People, places, things, as I've seen in the recovery literature. I'm hoping Cheryl will not go back to her boyfriend, and I'll encourage her to leave Kentucky and maybe come to Connecticut.

"We talk about relapse triggers all the time," Cheryl wrote me, "I know what to do to avoid them."

I add another column to my white board:

AVOID RELAPSE TRIGGERS

LETTER FROM CHERYL

September 2014

Thanks for the birthday wishes and the books.

Read LIFE OF PI, and now on to SOMEONE.

As birthdays go, this could be better.

But having you, a good book and the package of hostess cupcakes you bought me in the commissary helps tremendously! It feels like someone cares when I pick up my commissary order.

Thanks for helping me get my meds too.

My mitigation was denied. Can you help me follow up?

I appreciate your offer to help me get back on my feet

when I get out, but I really want to do it on my own.

I think it's important for my long-term recovery.

It helps to know you are there for me though.

Love,
Cheryl

CHERYL'S FACEBOOK POST

Cheryl   •••
January 22, 2011 1:27PM

I made amends for all my wrongs years ago,
now it's time to clear out the crap and let
those who have hurt me know they did, and
let them go . . . Good riddance, and bless my
true friends and family, they are priceless.

G-d bless everyone.

     👍 Like   ↪ Share

(Did she realize this was the anniversary date of the plane crash?)

WHAT PREGNANCY?

I'm not upset that you lied to me; I'm upset that from now on I can't believe you.

— FREDRICH NIETZSCHE

O N A PHONE CALL, I tell Cheryl that David and I are expecting our fourth grandchild. This will be the second child for his oldest son and his wife.

"She's doing well with this one, and she only has a little morning sickness," I say, mostly to make conversation.

"Or what I used to call all-day-sickness," Cheryl says with a sarcastic laugh.

I am shocked into momentary silence, but recover to ask, "What?

What do you mean? Were you ever —?"

"Oh, nothing, just kidding."

Seemingly on cue, the system announcement intrudes: *This call will end in 30 seconds.*

I have no time to regroup before we hang up.

In my next letter I ask, "Were you ever pregnant? When? What happened? Did your mom know?" I don't ask if she had the baby. Instead, I tell her I have friends who had abortions, thinking this might make her feel more comfortable confiding in me. But my questions go unanswered in subsequent letters. I'm afraid to ask on a phone call, worried she will just stop talking to me.

Would my sister have told me if Cheryl had been pregnant? It saddens me in a new way to realize I'm not sure. Linda held back details of her life that might upset me or reflect badly on her daughters. She told me very little when Cheryl first went to a rehab, and less during the times when Cheryl disappeared for months. Until it was absolutely dire, she never told me about needing money for groceries or rent. My parents helped for many years, until they didn't have the money to do it any longer. When it had become too difficult for Linda to go to a regular job because of problems with her hips and knees, she received disability payments and worked part-time at home as a medical transcriptionist. For the most part, she was able to piece together enough income for her needs, but it was a tight budget. She never complained, making do with a small apartment and second-hand furniture.

Not until I was writing *Replacement Child* did I approach my sister about our childhood. Probably the detachment of writing the book allowed me to dare dig into our family dynamic, along with the absolute necessity for the sake of the writing. I had been writing the book for two years and had not mentioned it to my sister, afraid of her questions and afraid she would think I was appropriating her story as my own. It wasn't until a point in the writing when I accepted *Replacement Child* was truly my story, about my own experiences as a child, that I talked to her about it. After admitting to Linda that I was indeed writing a book, I began our conversation by asking about logistics of our childhood home. What color were the kitchen appliances? What was the configuration of chairs in our family room? As we talked, Linda revealed my mother's affair with "Uncle" Jack. He was not our biological uncle, but the father of the girl my mother had saved from the burning apartment when the plane hit. She'd been visiting my sister, Donna, who died in the crash. Linda told me the affair started when both she and Uncle Jack were frequently at the hospital together, visiting their daughters. His daughter was also badly burned, though not as seriously as Linda. Linda reminded me how our father hated hospitals and was rarely there.

"Jack was there all the time, and they spent a lot of time together.

They even went away together once."

"Are you sure, really? I thought that was all just nothing, that his wife was kind of nuts and imagined he was having an affair with Mom."

"Don't you remember when Mom took us both to the city, without Dad?"

"Yes. I was little, but it felt weird."

"And Dad was waiting for us at the train station when we came home? When did he ever leave his store to come get us anywhere? She did not plan to go back, I know that."

My mother had confided in Linda and asked her to keep this secret from me. I felt myself recoil and try to deny it. I'm still trying to deny it.

"Then Uncle Jack bought that house on the street over from us, and joined our swim club, remember?"

I remembered, but never put it all together. Maybe I was oblivious because I was five years younger than Linda. Uncle Jack often brought us expensive gifts, igniting my father's anger. He gave Linda a mini TV for her bedroom after a surgery confined her to bed for a long recovery. My parents fought in their room, my father insisting the TV be returned. It was too big a gift to accept from a non-family member. My mother won that argument, because the TV made Linda's recovery so much easier. I never understood why my father bristled whenever Uncle Jack showed up. Jack's wife was never with him, and we were told something vague about her not being well.

Once, when I was six or so, Jack's wife burst into our house with accusations, which made no sense to my child brain. I watched, riveted, from the top of the staircase. My mother looked pale and on the verge of fainting and retreated to her bedroom while my father "handled" the situation and ushered the "crazy" woman out the door.

I asked Linda about this episode. "She wasn't crazy, she just found out about the affair."

My mother had been dead for three years by the time of this conversation, and Linda would die just a year later. She could just as easily have passed before ever telling me. What other secrets died with her?

THE LIFE

> You become a narcotics addict because you do not have strong motivations in any other direction. Junk wins by default. . . . . You don't decide to be an addict. One morning you wake up sick and you're an addict.

> — WILLIAM S. BURROUGHS
> *Junky*

WHAT LEADS TO ADDICTION? What is the life of an addict like? And how the hell can someone get out of it? Searching for answers, I turn to the notorious William S. Burroughs, author of *Junky* and *Naked Lunch*.

Junky, published in 1953, is a very journalistic read, chronicling Burroughs' daily life as a junky. Getting the "product"—either H (heroin) or M (morphine) or any combination available. Protecting and selling the product and navigating the related legal and social hurdles, often while in mortal danger. The high is always central in his daily life, nothing else even comes close. Leafing through the book, I find it tedious, boring, and terrifying. Burroughs' life was always on the brink.

The actual high diminishes with time. It gets to the point that the main reason to score is to prevent being dope-sick (flu-like symptoms of vomiting, diarrhea, aching, chills, anxiety). Withdrawal from opiates is very uncomfortable, but not usually life-threatening, as detoxing from alcohol can be. I try to imagine Cheryl in this mind-numbing cycle. I make myself finish reading *Junky* because I feel I should trudge through the experience like she has.

Naked Lunch is another story entirely. Acclaimed as a break-through book of its time, part of the Beat Generation of Kerouac and Ginsberg, I expect the lofty prose, but not the violence and ho-moerotic scenes, or the ones bordering on pedophilia. I do not finish the book. I just can't.

Watching Burroughs' interviews online from the 60s, I wince at the way he talks about addiction. "I don't regret my experience with drugs," he says, because it led to his writing success. His statement that "the damage to health is minimal, no matter what the American narcotics department may say," is repeated word for word in three of the interviews I find. He seems to truly believe his claim, in denial of the facts concerning health and drug use.

The interviewers don't refute this erroneous information, and I wonder why.

The National Institute of Health (NIH) lists numerous health issues caused by opiates, including diseases of the liver, lungs and heart, along with risk of Hepatitis C and HIV—to name just a few. An infection of the heart called cardiac endocarditis, for example, can be a direct result of intravenous drug use. The NIH notes addiction also affects brain function, including behavior control—which seems like a cruel joke. You can't stop because you can't stop.

I might give Burroughs the benefit of the doubt in purporting the minimal harm of addiction because of the time period in which he lived. Or maybe he was in denial of his own dependency. My anger is around his being revered as a cult hero, glorifying the legacy of addiction, and building a cornerstone for the next generation's drug culture. Burroughs, I conclude, was a danger to society, and an asshole.

LETTER FROM CHERYL

October 2014

Just finished re-reading your book, and it's helping me look at some of my issues.

Mom just struggled to have a normal life, and I was handed it on a silver platter and I throw it away.

Makes me pretty ashamed.

Love,
Cheryl

BEFORE YOU
WERE YOU

Stress has everything to do with addiction. . . .The physiological stress response involves nervous discharges throughout the body and the release of a cascade of hormones, chiefly adrenaline and cortisol. . . stresses during pregnancy can already begin to "program" predisposition to addiction in the developing human being.

— GABOR MATÉ
In the Realm of Hungry Ghosts

CHERYL SAYS SHE WAS GIVEN EVERYTHING, and she threw it away. She misconstrues the narrative of our family's suffering in my book and turns it into a new way to attack herself. I am beginning to understand the depth of her feeling of unworthiness, and why she has a hard time asking for help. She doesn't believe she deserves it. Even so, she says she will survive and climb back up. I want to believe this so much.

When I read her letters, I think about her unassuming voice on the phone. The way she apologizes for bothering me. For calling. For asking for commissary money. For her handwriting. How can I make her feel worthy?

As a child, Cheryl always had a roof over her head, plenty of food, a mother who loved her and loving grandparents. Even with her parents' divorce, the picture of a stable, supportive childhood lodges in my mind. When I spoke to her dad after I discovered Cheryl in jail, he said everything came easy to her when she was young. She got good grades without trying.

"So smart," Phil's voice lowered as he remembered. "She seemed like she would sail through."

I can still see her roller-skating down the street, holding tight to Debbie's hand. That smile. Until something happened. Why didn't I see the storm warning? Did her mother?

I used to blame Linda's move to Florida for Cheryl's problems. I felt the education system in Florida didn't measure up to standards in the northeast. I cringed when I saw the kids attending classes in a trailer school room. It's also one reason I never thought of moving to Florida, even when I had no family in Connecticut. Justin's education was my primary concern, I told my parents, without admitting my fear of drowning in the undertow of their chaos.

When Linda moved so far from her children's father, I thought it was unfair to Phil. I didn't know then what stopped me from saying so, but now I think it was the hallowed space my sister occupied in our family. The physical distance between Linda and Phil made it difficult for the kids to see their dad and began years of arguments about visits and child support.

"She never sent the kids up to see me," Phil complains still.

Linda said she was frustrated he never sent enough money for things the kids needed or was late with support payments. He tells me he put aside money for both girls over the years and gave it to them when they turned 21. As in most divorces, it's complicated. I only know what each has told me.

Family history and biology need to be considered as I try to understand where Cheryl has landed.

We now know that trauma can fuse biology and family history. The very way hormones act on our genes is affected by trauma,[8] and this hormone performance can be passed down through generations. So it's not a gene for addiction or alcoholism per se that is handed down, but the way certain chemicals attach themselves to DNA and affect how a gene acts, or gene expression. This gene expression is called transgenerational epigenetic inheritance.

A classic example of epigenetics is how a mother rat licks her pup shortly after it's born, which turns on a gene in the brain that keeps the pup from being overwhelmed by stress throughout its life.[9] In the same way, trauma can also be inherited. The work of Rachel

Yehuda, professor of psychiatry and neuroscience at Mount Sinai School of Medicine in New York, and one of the world's leading experts on PTSD, reinforces these findings. Also relevant is her research on cortisol, the stress hormone that helps the body recover and return to normal after a trauma. Her work has transformed the way PTSD is understood and treated. From her extensive studies with Holocaust survivors and their children, war veterans, and mothers who were pregnant during 911 and their children, she has found trauma survivors and their children all show *low* blood levels of the essential cortisol. Interestingly, this conflicts with previously held views of PTSD being associated with *high* levels of cortisol. But her research clarified that chronic pain syndrome, chronic fatigue syndrome, major depression, and PTSD, are all associated with low cortisol levels.[10] It's another way trauma can be handed down from generation to generation.

Like many Jews, my family came to this country near the turn of the twentieth century to escape the pogroms in Russia and anti-Jewish actions in Hungary. We lost many relatives to the Holocaust. But I don't need to go back that far for a source of our trauma. The plane crash in 1952 that killed my older sister and gravely injured Linda is the traumatic event I believe trickled down through my mother, my sister, her daughters—and me.

The prenatal, as well as postnatal, environment contributes to the way genes function in humans. If a mother is under stress, or experiences trauma during pregnancy, the fetus is bathed in the stress hormone cortisol. Much of Linda's life was stressful, painful or traumatic in one way or another, making me wonder if Cheryl's path was somewhat pre-programmed well before she was born.

Likewise, the physical development of a fetus is also affected by a mother's stress. Maté says, *"Cortisol itself acts on the tissues of almost every part of the body—from the brain to the immune system, from the bones to the intestines."*[11]

This information hits me in a totally different way, with the knowledge we all (me, my sister and our kids) are also part of this equation of transgenerational trauma.

There is no doubt that my mother was under tremendous stress while pregnant with me, shortly after the plane crash. She was grieving for her older daughter and caring for her gravely injured little girl. How was my own biology affected by a likely flood of cortisol in utero? Perhaps weakening my immune system and contributing to my Crohn's Disease.

Turning to the nurture part of the equation, my parents' insistence that Linda was as normal as any other kid was well-meaning but didn't take into account reactions from the world outside our home. Psychological counseling was not the norm, and Dad thought "head shrinkers" were a waste of money. Or maybe he just couldn't afford it. I can't help thinking of the father in Eugene O'Neill's *Long Day's Journey into Night* saying to his son Edmund when he is diagnosed with TB, "You can go anywhere you want (for the cure), within reason—that I can afford."

Linda loved her daughters very much, but there was an element of instability in their household.

We may not be so different from families who survived the Holocaust, the tentacles of trauma reaching down through the generations.

Cheryl may be right that she was "given everything."

White board additions:

EPIGENETIC HEREDITY

TRANSGENERATIONAL TRAUMA

CHERYL'S FACEBOOK POST

Cheryl ...
September 21, 2011 9:56PM

Hey y'all. . . Ur fav reclusive fb shunner here to actually give an update! It's amazing what you can get done when ur not on fb all the time! We are doin fine, workin too hard, playin too little, loving our chaotic little zoo family we've created. Health issues abound as always so I won't bore you there . . . (Ok, maybe a lil . . . I lost a couple of pounds and an ovary! Jd's foot is healed and he's walking, but always pain, and def more surgery in his future) hope we can get out to hang with our friends soon . . . And looking forward to a fam visit in a couple of weeks (YAY!). I'm thinking I need a concert, and im thinking we all need to go to 80's nite at Atlantis skateway! Lol com on u know u want to! Luv all y'all—

👍 Like   ⤳ Share

At the time of this post, two years after her mother died, Cheryl had a steady job as an office manager and lived with her long-time boyfriend in a small house in West Palm Beach. They had taken in her mom's tiny dog, adding to their lab and two cats. She never mentioned the removal of her ovary to me, and this look at archived posts is the first I know of it. I think my visit was the "fam visit" she mentions.

This post seems odd now, with its southern lilt and overly upbeat tone.

LETTER FROM CHERYL

November 2014

They started giving me my Selexca [sic], thanks to you.

I hope that's enough to get me through. It's definitely better than nothing.

I can tell the anti-depressants are wearing off, and I hope the Selexca kicks in in a week or so.

There's no program or counselor here.

Not much else to report now.

Love always,

Cheryl

WHO SURVIVES?

The mentality and behaviour of drug addicts and
alcoholics is wholly irrational until you understand that
they are completely powerless over their addiction and
unless they have structured help they have no hope.

— RUSSELL BRAND

WHY CAN SOME PEOPLE BEAT ADDICTION, and others can't?
Many books by ex-addicts talk about a combination of 12-
Step programs and family support. But even people with both may
not recover. It seems like having support is crucial, and it sends me
down the rabbit hole of wondering if I am giving Cheryl enough.

The news of Philip Seymour Hoffman's death takes me by the
shoulders and shakes me. He was found dead in his apartment with
a needle in his arm. Hoffman had reportedly been sober for two

decades. He was in the midst of a creative blitz of successful movies and working on a play. It's hard to imagine that he was bored with his life. Some say he may have been the best actor of our time. Why did he need those 70 bags of heroin found in his apartment? Also found were prescriptions for buprenorphine, a drug used to ease withdrawal. Apparently, he knew how to detox and may have done it recently. There was conjecture he may have overdosed with his usual dose when his tolerance was diminished after detoxing, which often occurs. Studies have shown that the more intelligent an addict, the less likely he is to recover. Did Hoffman believe he could outsmart his addiction by alternating between detoxing and using? If someone like him can't survive, will Cheryl be able to rebuild her life and beat her addiction? Hoffman's death opens a new fault-line of fear.

Other research shows addicts may be trying to relieve stress resulting from a biochemical imbalance in the brain, depression, PTSD, bipolar or other disorders. Physicians specializing in addiction customize treatment to the individual. They utilize several different approaches including medication, talk therapy, body work (like Yoga), neurofeedback and EMDR (Eye Movement Desensitization and Reprocessing). Finding the right treatment for recovery is a challenge in itself. There is an entire industry built around bogus rehab centers that promise a total cure and rarely deliver. I file away this knowledge to tap in the future.

I am at a loss to understand why Russell Brand could recover and Hoffman could not. Even more, I am concerned by Cheryl's dismissal of the 12-Step program, which is the most accessible form of support in prison.

White board additions:

PRE-EXISTING CONDITIONS

12-STEPS

NEW TREATMENTS

FAMILY SUPPORT

LETTER TO CHERYL

NOVEMBER 2014

I've been thinking about when you get out, and reading more about addiction and relapse.

You and I have both learned a lot about it by now.

Hopefully you will cut ties with anyone from that past.

That's one reason I offered to come and help you get situated when you get out, or have you come here.

This is a second chance for you and I really want you to make a break with that past life.

I realize I am talking from a place of not truly understanding—but I am trying.

I imagine how difficult it is to think about re-inventing your life.

But you have to create a new future if you are going to survive.

LY,
Aunt Judy

LETTER FROM CHERYL

December 2014

Started getting my aspirin again for my blood condition.

I can't believe you were able to get me my meds.

Thinking now about what I'll do when I'm released.

Hard to plan because Parole may have other ideas for me.

They have to approve my home placement, or pick a halfway house (okay option), or the Salvation Army (homeless shelter—not okay!)

I'm sure we will talk soon and I'll have more news now that I only have a short time left.

LY,
Cheryl

LETTER TO CHERYL

DECEMBER 2014

Dear Cher,

I am excited/nervous for you going to a halfway house. I have no idea what that is like.

Maybe I can come for a visit and stay nearby? Take you for a few meals, and see if you need anything?

What do you think?

I really would love to see you, it's been years now— and I'm not getting any younger!

You sounded good on the phone this week. Glad you are keeping busy.

The next phase is coming quickly and you will be out of there and on to your new life!

I love you very much!

AJ

THE HEALING
PLACE

There is a crack in everything,

that's how the light gets in.

— LEONARD COHEN

FROM THE WINDOW OF MY HOTEL IN LOUISVILLE, I scan the view of low, flat factory buildings. Roofs so flat you could land a helicopter. A scattering of ornate architecture catches my eye, with crowns of sculpted diamonds, fanned seashells and fearsome gargoyles.

The Brown Hotel is like a horse museum. Paintings of horses grazing in open green fields contained by low white fences. Cartoon horses bucking under a rider holding on for dear life. Bronze horses, posing like proud heads of state. Racehorses crossing the Derby finish line.

As I was checking in, the conversations around me were all about sports, horses, or food. Where to get the best Hot Browns—here, of course. Fried chicken? The Colonel's or his wife's restaurant, Claudia's Place? But I am not here on vacation or a business trip.

I drop my bags in my room and text Cheryl that I'm here. She was released from prison a few weeks ago and is at a halfway house called The Healing Place for Women.

Can't wait to see you, she texts back.

Me too, I reply, though I'm feeling anxious at seeing her for the first time in four years.

It's mid-afternoon by the time I get into my rental car and follow the directions she has given me. This section of the city seems to be racing away from its past. Neon lures the eye to pawn shops, maniacally situated next to liquor stores. One lone discount clothing store showcases identical boxy blouses. No Starbucks. No Dunkin' Donuts. One McDonald's around the corner and a Walgreens nearby. Wide streets have mild traffic. An occasional ambulance, its siren blaring toward one of the city's three hospitals.

Silent factories and blank-faced buildings line the desolate streets. A man in a black hoodie, scraggly black beard, hands in pockets, saunters across the street in front of an oncoming car that brakes into a skid. He hardly notices.

GPS orders me to *turn left in 500 feet … turn left … turn left*. At the corner of another bleak street, a black iron fence cordons off a low brick building. I spot the sign for The Healing Place. Wide windows on its two floors reveal a busy facility. I park, take a deep breath, and text Cheryl, **I'm here!**

Inside, bustling with tasks and purpose are girls as young as teens and women much older than my forty-year-old niece. I know from Cheryl some are just getting through detox. Others are further along in the recovery program, or like her, have served a jail sentence and are here to transition back to a real life, if they can find one.

I approach the double glass door and peer in. It looks like my old college dorm. As I walk in, three young women shout at me from the far corners of the hexagonal entryway.

"You can't go in there."

"She can't go in there!"

"Stop!"

How threatening do I look, I wonder? A near sixty-year-old 5'2" woman in a parka? The girl who is now half-standing at the check-in desk can't be more than twenty, and maybe 100 pounds. I can't help thinking of this girl's mother.

I stop, but glance in at the living area. Clean edges. White linoleum floor. Tiny alcoves with a set of bunk beds, one drawer, six hangers on a metal bar. Where will Cheryl put the new jacket I brought her to keep warm in the coldest January here in decades? Hers was threadbare, she wrote. My sister wouldn't forgive me if I let her daughter freeze out here while she scrambles to pull her life back together. I spot her inside, her familiar gait, her smile so like her mother's. The shock of the incongruity of seeing her in this place causes an involuntary gasp, which I cover with a cough.

The last time I saw her we were still grieving her mother's death. She had become somewhat domestic in her little house in Florida, organizing spices and trying out recipes her grandmother—my mother—had given her. I had brought her some silverware as a gift when I saw she had only mismatched spoons and forks. As she comes through the door now, I notice first how her skin has changed from the youthful smoothness I remember to a more weathered texture. She roughly tells the desk girl, "She's with me," then softens as she comes to give me a hug.

Don't look away. See this. It's happening. Don't just go back to safe suburban Connecticut. Or drive to Starbucks to write. I hate you for that. Be here now. Do something!

I have a history of looking away. My sister, as much as I loved her, was for me a black hole of need I feared would swallow me. There was always something—some romantic drama, some medical issue, some financial dilemma. She was courageous, though, facing a world that instantly judges based on the superficial; her scars the first impression many didn't look past. As we drifted away from each other, and lived increasingly further apart, I was engrossed in my own life. There were times I'd send a little money, some item she needed, or a round of groceries, but in the back of my mind I thought, *I can never do enough.* My last regret is that I did nothing to dissuade her from entering an experimental drug program for her chronic pain a year before she died. A drug regimen I now believe weakened her and contributed to her death. She'd also asked for help to buy the new electronic cigarette to help her quit her two-pack-a-day habit, which I did not do—citing it as experimental, from the research I'd read. Maybe if I had, her lung cancer would have been kept at bay. Maybe if I had moved her from the apartment with the awful ventilation, maybe it would have saved her. *Maybe, maybe, maybe.*

I share my misgivings with my niece, as we sit over a sumptuous Hot Brown platter at its namesake hotel. French toast, bacon, tomato, turkey, open-faced with cheese-sauce gravy. We laugh that we'll need a nap afterward, and maybe a coronary bypass.

"That place was terrible," she says of her mother's last apartment. "She was breathing in all that smoke."

"I cleaned the air filter once, and it was black with soot. But only once. I never went back to do it again. Then she moved, just before she got sick."

"I should have done it too."

Cheryl takes out an e-cigarette, holding it exactly the way her mother would. She says it has much less nicotine than cigarettes and is helping her quit. The vapor isn't offensive, she says. And it's not, but I still have to stifle bile-inducing anger at the very act of her smoking, picturing my sister's last gasp before lung cancer claimed her life.

As Cheryl smokes and I concentrate on my iced tea, she tells me, "The rehab program was good in Ohio, but there wasn't much of one when they transferred me to Kentucky."

"I was glad you had at least one." I'm tense at the introduction of this topic, and I don't ask about the program at The Healing Place, though I know they have one.

"It helped me figure out some things about myself, and the anti-depressants really do help."

I stir my tea, take a sip, and don't probe this point.

We talk about keeping up her medications and prescription coverage. In her eyes I see how hard it all is. Finally, I ignore the tightening in my chest and force myself to ask about getting into a program and suggest she go to some meetings.

"It's not for me, Aunt Judy. I'm good now. I'll never go back to that life. Believe me." More than anything, I want to believe her, and I drop it.

I'm glad to hear that her sister has texted with her a bit since she now has an "Obama phone." We don't talk about their past arguments.

I want to solve everything in the three days I have with her. We run into obstacles with banking, medications, healthcare. She's quick to say, "No worries, I'll figure it out." She laughs like the little girl I remember, the guttural belly laugh like her mother's. I see she is trying to ease my concerns. I have no idea how she will figure any of it out. With twenty years on her, and a stable life, I can't fathom putting all this together. All I can do is buy that jacket, a couple of sweaters, and supplies at the drug store. She is so grateful and seems like her old self as we talk about her mom over our Hot Browns.

She downs two Diet Pepsis while I nurse my tea. We sit in the ornate hotel lobby bar for our meal, marveling at the art. Every inch of wall and ceiling is decorated with carvings and paintings. Antique armoires line the walls. The bar counter is a work of art, cut from one piece of beautiful maple. The place seems to have an eerie nostalgic vibe of the Old South. Our waiter eyes my plate and tells me I have plenty of time to finish.

"We're here 'til two a.m. ma'am, no rush," he says. Finally, I push it away, unable to swallow another bite. Cheryl finishes hers quickly.

"I appreciate meat," she tells me.

We go up to my room to use the hair color we bought at the drug store to cover her gray roots. I offer to help, but she declines. I busy myself with my laptop, searching for banks that may give her an account. I see this as a necessity for her to move forward. In the end, after calling five banks and visiting two, it's a futile effort and I feel overwhelmed. She is on their list and nothing I say dissuades them.

My mind drifts to the praying hands necklace my sister always wore, engraved with the Serenity prayer:

God grant me the serenity to accept the things I cannot change, courage to change the things I can, and the wisdom to know the difference.

Like my sister, I lean on that message now.

Sitting on the bed with her hair up in a towel, making her look much younger, my niece tells me she took her mom to the ER on several occasions for withdrawal from pain medication. This, I never knew. But I knew she was in constant pain after a botched knee replacement. Doctors told her it couldn't be redone because of scar tissue from her burns.

Our conversation opens a seam in the fabric of my inner story. It seems my sister never really talked to me about what was going on in her life. Maybe my ideas about her were some kind of fantasy. In my mind, she remained "our little soldier" as my parents called her each time she went into the hospital.

Linda wouldn't use her cane when I came to visit. She would

hobble to the door to greet me, then drop with a thud into the closest chair, the cane leaning up against the molding behind the front door. We'd always end up laughing about something from our childhood, like the doghouse we built together from leftover roof shingles—too small for the dog and so heavy we couldn't move it. Or the hair-dye job in high school that left her with clownish orange hair. And how she scared me again and again by hiding and jumping out from behind the couch after we watched the movie *Wait Until Dark*. Her laugh is something I miss every day. No one has ever laughed so readily at my jokes, or with her full belly laugh—so much like Cheryl's. *Remember when* about my childhood is something I can no longer say to anyone.

I wipe the tears away and look over to see Cheryl doing the same.

On my last night with her, we find it hard to say goodbye in the parking lot of The Healing Place. We sit in the car for a half hour, until curfew, talking about her plans. To find a permanent job, a way to keep her weekly pay safe, to get her meds and health coverage. I know the list is too much for her.

"My offer still holds for you to come stay with me for a while, you know," I tell her, fighting the twist of fear in my belly at the prospect.

"I have to do it on my own, really, it's better for my recovery."

I wonder if that is the real reason, but don't challenge her, and I hope she can't detect my relief.

Finally, our time has run out and we both get out of the car. I hand her the bag of supplies we picked up at Walgreens and she winds the plastic handle between her fingers. We hug for a long moment, and I take her hand and walk her to the door. I watch her sign in and walk into her alcove and I don't leave until I lose sight of her. In my mind I follow her to the upper bunk, see her unpack the bag of toiletries and find a place to put them out of sight, hang her new jacket and tuck her new boots between the covers.

The next week she will write that the boots were stolen within a day.

That evening, I laid my suitcase across the chenille bedspread that reminds me of my mother's, under an intricate Derby painting of a photo finish, the lead horse straining its rippled neck to cross the line by a nose. I toast the winner with the bourbon I feel obliged to try before leaving Kentucky, which scalds both my throat and sinuses. As I pack my things, I catch sight of a sunset blasting orange and red, reflecting on a slender strip of the Ohio River, momentarily lighting up the gray city.

FEBRUARY TO MAY

So we beat on, boats against the current, borne back
ceaselessly into the past.

— F. SCOTT FITZGERALD

Between February and May 2015, deadlines for my late-in-
life master's degree take up most of my time. I find I have
much less patience for the academic bureaucracy I thought I'd left
behind some 40 years ago. There have been several moments when
I've nearly quit, even now, near the end of my studies.

Cheryl and I talk once a week. I tell her how I am working hard
on my thesis, but I don't mention it's a novel about a young woman
who becomes addicted to cocaine. Maybe I am trying to ferret out

truth within my fiction, creating a character I can control in order to find a path for Cheryl.

Graduation ceremonies are two-fold, one in Southampton with my small writing class, and the larger Stony Brook University extravaganza. One good friend from the program decides to join me for the big event, wanting the whole pageantry of the occasion. We are both excited Billy Joel is speaking, though we'd rather he sing.

David and I check in to a hotel on the campus the night before the ceremony and order champagne and strawberries for a small celebration. My son drives through the night from Georgia to be here—a reversal of roles that tickles me. Getting this degree at 60 is a milestone I wasn't sure I would reach. Hell, I wasn't sure I would even survive the last few years, having come close to death three times with emergency surgeries and complications from Crohn's Disease. Blocking out the one certain truth that we will die is the greatest feat of suspended disbelief we humans continuously maintain, until something comes along to shock us out of our fantasy. Nearly dying made this accomplishment all the sweeter.

The event itself is a marathon of waiting and marching. We pose for many pictures together, me in my cap and gown with the special collar for the master's degree. I catch my husband with watery eyes, a rare sighting. My son hugs me tightly, "I'm so proud of you, Mama," he whispers. My friend, an older student too, has brought her three children and husband. We share an understanding of the poignancy of our late accomplishment as we take pictures together like all the 20-somethings swarming the campus on this hot day in May, which just happens to be my birthday. Still, there is an undercurrent of guilt that I recognize. In the past, it was when my life was going well and my sister's was not. Now Cheryl is that pebble in my shoe.

My conversations with Cheryl are short now, to save her phone minutes. We talk about ways to get her medical care for depression and Hepatitis C. Obamacare coverage, literally a lifeline, pays for all her doctor visits and prescriptions. Although the next election is now in view, it looks like Hillary will easily win, since the Republican line-up seems to be filled with ludicrous candidates. I believe Hillary will improve health care for people who really need help—like Cheryl.

Cheryl's "Obama phone" is free to those who meet the income requirements. It has limited minutes and data, but it's more than she would be able to get on her own and lets us stay in touch. I don't want to lose our connection again. More than ever, I'm grateful to President Obama who obviously cares about people and makes their lives better.

Cheryl tells me she is working, trying to turn her temp job at the pillow factory into full time, and living with a friend from The Healing Place.

"It feels good to be doing physical work," she says.

Cheryl is making her way and surviving on her own. Yes, she is too smart to be packing boxes on a conveyor line, but the felony on her record makes it nearly impossible to get another office manager position. We plan to try to have her record expunged, which is possible after a year of no arrests. It will require several letters of recommendation; difficult documentation when you don't have a computer at your disposal. I also suggest finding one of the employers that are paid a supplement from the government to hire people with felonies, but she says she is happy where she is.

Even so, David and I discuss how to help Cheryl get a better job, and he makes some calls at his company. It turns out the company has a distribution center in Louisville, and he arranges an interview. She and I polish her resume, and I coach her on how to handle the interview, role playing on the phone.

I tell her, "Just be as honest as you can possibly be. Don't try to hide anything, because your record is easy to find."

When the day comes, I text her to see how it went.

I couldn't make it.

What happened?

My shift ran late, and I couldn't get there.

Did you call them to explain?

I want to give her every benefit of doubt.

Yes.

No, she did not call them, David finds out from his Human Resources contact. And, no, they will not reschedule the appointment.

SHOT

I N JUNE I GET A FRANTIC TEXT FROM CHERYL.

We got shot at last night! I was sitting on the steps right next to where the bullet came.

She texts a photo of a small round hole next to the front door of the house where she rents a room.

When I call her, she sounds shaken.

"It came out of nowhere!"

"Did you see anyone? Did you call the police?" No and no.

It's the first picture I've seen of the house where she lives. A faded yellow clapboard with peeling paint. A ripped screen door. Cracked cement steps. The bullet hole seems at home. A wave of guilt hits me.

How can I let her live there? Yet, I remember, she wanted to stay in Louisville.

"I have to move, I can't stay here," she tells me.

"Where else can you look for a place? Is your roommate still living there?"

Not knowing the neighborhood or the proximity to her workplace, I am not much help looking for a new place.

All I had were questions, and I didn't get many answers.

"I'll figure it out."

What I didn't know was that she also called her old boyfriend, James. The one she lived with just before her arrest, who was now out on parole in Ohio. I assumed they had a common history of drug use. After a month of not hearing from her, she tells me she begged him to come stay with her after the shooting. I understand how scared she was, but I am sure this is not the man to protect her from anything, and his arrival just gives me another source of concern.

It isn't long before he is arrested for skipping parole and is back in jail.

Now that she is alone again, she calls and texts more frequently. It's evident she's waiting for him to get out. She hates being alone. I hold my breath. But she sounds good on the phone, like her old self, and I tell myself people change.

CHERYL'S FACEBOOK POST

Cheryl

June 11, 2015 10:05AM

I can finally look in a mirror and see that I am a beautiful woman inside and out, and I won't let anyone take that away from me ever again.

👍 Like   ↪ Share

RED FLAG

ON CHERYL'S BIRTHDAY, when I call to wish her a good one, she asks me to please order her a pizza as a birthday gift. "I'm running short on money, and it would be really great to have a real meal for my birthday."

She has no money for food? How did this happen?

A slow-down at work, she says. Not enough hours this week.

Something has stopped me from sending her cash directly, an internal warning against giving her easy means to buy drugs. If anyone asks me, I tell them I believe she is clean, but there must be an unconscious blink still in play. Pizza is another thing.

She gives me the number for the local Pizza Hut, and I order everything I think she might like: a large pepperoni pizza, stuffed bread, bottle of soda, chocolate dessert. She texts me when it arrives.

Thank you so much Aunt Judy! You made my birthday!

Such a small thing. But also a red flag. She had no money for a damn pizza? I imagine her eating the pizza straight out of the box and drinking soda from the bottle on her bed in the small room she rents, with the shared bath and kitchen. In my mind I see her mother's worried face, begging me to be vigilant for her child.

SISTER MY SISTER

Oh sister, when I come to lie in your arms,
You should not treat me like a stranger.
Oh sister, when I come to knock on your door,
Don't turn away, you'll create sorrow.

— BOB DYLAN

Oh, Sister

I TALK TO MY DEAD SISTER, LINDA, A LOT LATELY. Asking for her advice. For forgiveness for not knowing the right steps to take with Cheryl. Should I insist that her daughter come live with me? Send her money? Believe her when she tells me, "Drugs are in my past"? Accept it when she says, "Meetings are not for me"? Sometimes I have vivid dreams of my sister: her soft beseeching eyes, her gentle touch reaching for my hand, but she never gives me any answers.

Understanding where addiction comes from doesn't help me understand where Cheryl is on her journey. My reading and talking to others with family members who struggle with addiction has taught me not to trust her. That I may never be able to trust her. How do I support her without enabling her? How do I love her while keeping my distance? A dilemma that feels oddly familiar.

Thinking of my own son, I try to reverse the situation, imagining I am gone, and Justin is in trouble. This doesn't help as much as I'd hoped. What would Linda have done in my place? She struggled to know how to help Cheryl. Sent her to rehabs, searched for her in unspeakable places, took her in, threw her out. I am a little pissed off that she died and left me to figure out how to help her daughter, after never really being honest with me about the depth of Cheryl's problems.

Oh sister. It was complicated, wasn't it? My appearing after your big sister was taken from you so suddenly. Filling a void but opening a new one. I never really understood your very private pain, because you never truly let me in. Through it all, though, I felt the force of your love, as I hope you felt from me. Even with you gone, I am left to untangle the threads of our story.

JULY 28, 2016

I WATCH EVERY MINUTE of the Democratic National Convention and cry when Hillary takes the stage. She looks ethereal and confident, almost angelic in her white pantsuit. A woman in control. I don't care what people say about "baggage"—who doesn't have baggage in the contentious world of politics? And most of her baggage was packed by men. Her record of humanitarian work, both as a private citizen, as First Lady and then Secretary of State, proves her mettle. I am definitely With Her.

Some of my friends are in the celebratory crowd in Brooklyn after the convention, and I scream along with them in front of the TV. The only other time I felt this impassioned and hopeful for our country was when Obama was elected. I vividly remember the shouts of excitement in our neighborhood, my neighbors coming out of their houses to share the joy in the streets. We seem on an upward spiral now, becoming more progressive and inclusive. Obama made strides in human rights and healthcare—and now I feel they will continue. It's amazing to consider. I can't help thinking how my parents would have reacted to a woman president—my mother in reverie, my dad in disbelief.

Looking out my front window the next day, onto a quiet green tree-lined street, I gaze lovingly at my Hillary Clinton for President sign that I pressed into the grass with the heel of my sneaker a few minutes ago. A smile creeps in and can't help itself. I am going to see the first woman president of the United States elected! It's about time! I notice a small rip in the corner of the plastic sign and rush out with tape to repair it.

Standing back off the curb to view the sign, I let out a sigh, seeing it fixed and positioned in the center of my lawn. My cell phone interrupts my daydream. It's Cheryl, calling to tell me she's met someone.

"Finally, Aunt Judy, a good guy with a job and a house," she says. She is so happy to give me good news, which fits with my own elevated mood.

Later, I find a picture of her on Facebook in his backyard pool. Her hair slicked back, wet from her swim, the happy-faced girl I remember. She is still in there.

When she calls the next week in a newly hopeful voice, she tells me her new boyfriend is the assignment manager at the temp agency. When I voice concern about a possible conflict, she pooh-poohs me.

"No, that means he can always get me work! Aunt Judy, I feel happier than I have in years. Be happy for me!"

Why does this feel like hearing a crack in a ceiling beam in the middle of the night? Is the roof caving in, or is the house just settling? She'd said these very words when she fled to Ohio in a stolen truck.

CHERYL'S FACEBOOK POST

Cheryl   •••
July 7, 2016 1:05PM

Life is as good as u want it to be . . .i finally stopped reaching down for dirt, and started reaching for the stars.

Pool party tomorrow, PM me.

Started working at Horseshoe Casino Southern Indiana!

👍 Like   ⤳ Share

NOVEMBER 8, 2016

Oh my fucking God!
– ME

T HE NIGHT OF THE ELECTION, David and I head to the local
Chili's where they are serving margaritas in special shakers to
mark the occasion. The shakers are just the usual blue plastic cups
emblazoned with Election 2016, but I figure it will be my memento
for this historic election of the first woman President of the United
States. Just last week, Cheryl and I were sharing our relief that Hillary will continue the Affordable Care Act, which Cheryl relies on.

I'm still proudly wearing an "I Voted" sticker on my jacket. Arriving around 6:30, we take a seat at the bar, where we can watch the
returns, smiling at our compatriots on adjacent stools. Three TVs are

tuned to different stations. We are in a jovial mood, and it seems we are in the company of others who feel the same. There is no doubt in our minds Trump has ruined his chances with the Access Hollywood tape and his other incredibly misogynistic and disgusting displays: mocking a disabled reporter, giving disparaging nicknames to all his opponents, dismissing as liars the multitude of women who have now accused him of sexual assault. He has no experience whatsoever in public service. His only service has been to his own bottom line, with a reputation in New York as an unscrupulous real estate mogul who evades taxes and manipulates the press. It's unthinkable how anyone could choose him over Hillary, who has been working for the public good all her life.

As the returns roll in, we are getting mildly discouraged, but assure each other it's early. Hillary can come back from an early deficit in the Electoral College. See, her popular vote is steadily ahead! When Michigan turns to Trump, we order more margaritas. Pennsylvania is a blow. What the fuck is happening?! Now I want to go home. The mood has shifted in the bar and people are visibly shaken, more than the margaritas. Many are leaning on their elbows, their heads in their hands. Some, me, are cursing with each checkmark under Trump's name on the scoreboard. By 9:00, the crowd has thinned, we pat some of our new friends on the back as we leave, saying, "There's still time."

At home I turn on the TV to watch the end of the devastating results. I watch until it's all but certain Trump has won. It's an Electoral College win, just like Bush, and I can't believe we still have this outdated system for choosing our leader. I get up and pace while the anchors at MSNBC drone on and on. CNN is no different. I am not even switching to FOX. That would be like pouring salt in the open wound. David has turned over and gone to sleep! How can he do that?! Finally, around 1:30 a.m., I go to the kitchen and pour myself a bourbon. A big one.

The next day I call Cheryl. With Trump's win, we discuss how to get all her needed medical tests, treatments and prescriptions before things may change in January. First on our list is to schedule doctors' appointments right away for her Hepatitis C, blood disorder, and her depression. Tomorrow she'll schedule the MRI and CT scan recommended for her back pain. I hear the fear in her voice when she assures me, "It will be okay, don't worry."

WHITE FLAG

T HE HOLIDAY RUSH OF BUYING PRESENTS for our four grandchildren and planning family visits is in full swing a couple
of weeks before Christmas when I get a text from Cheryl's sister,
Debbie:

Cheryl is sick and needs help.

I've heard very little from Cheryl since November. When I tried
calling, I got a message the number was no longer in service.

She has a new phone number again.

Debbie texts me the number.

What's wrong?

> She's staying in a house alone with
> no heat and says she is sick.

Last I knew she was living in a house
with some friends.

> They left when they couldn't pay the
> heat bill. It's really cold there now. I
> don't know what to do, Aunt Judy.

I call Cheryl's new number.

She tells me she tried to stay in the house with no heat, but it got too cold, so she is looking for a place to stay. Her voice is shaky.

"I'm not doing so good here. Can I come stay there for a while?"

Instinctively I know things have all gone wrong. What happened to the job she'd told me turned permanent? What happened to the boyfriend who could always get her work? What happened? There are too many questions, and she says her allotted minutes on her Obama Phone are running out, so I focus on the issue of her immediate safety.

"Let's find a warm place for you to stay first," I tell her.

The shelters are all full, but if the temperature dips below freezing, Cheryl tells me, "They have to let you in." It's called White Flag, when the weather is life-threatening and places like the Salvation Army and the Mission open their doors whether or not they have a bed. A surrender to the elements and to the reality that turning people away in sub-freezing temperatures is tantamount to murder. A surrender on the part of the homeless too, who are forced to seek any kind of shelter that will take them. Right now, it's hovering just above the freezing mark. But it's still too cold to be without heat. Cheryl is coughing and sniffling as she explains.

I get busy online looking for affordable hotels while I get a grasp on the situation. There is one near her with breakfast included and I make her a reservation for three nights, adding in their dinner buffet. It is already 4:00 in the afternoon and I don't want her to have another cold night. "Call me when you get there."

When she arrives at the hotel and gives her name for the reservation, the desk clerk has her call me to verify the reservation. I have a feeling it has something to do with the way Cheryl looks. I confirm and tell them to charge my credit card, including the dinners.

"I'm sorry, Aunt Judy, I know this is all a pain. Thank you for helping me. I've really been trying, but things are not going well for me here. And I have some kind of stomach virus and a really bad cold and am pretty sick."

As much as I try, I can't help thinking of the descriptions of dope-sick I've read—*like having the flu, diarrhea, vomiting.*

After a good night's sleep, she sounds much better the next morning. She confides she doesn't have a job now—and I already know she doesn't have a place to stay.

"Things are just not working out here," she says again.

"A job and a place to live—let's concentrate on that."

I tell her I'll call her twice each day. In the morning to plan her day, to make some progress, in the evening to see how she made out. She knows of a place in Louisville where there is help to find work and housing, and she goes there the first day. I start looking on Craigslist for jobs and rooms to rent.

In a quick conversation, because her minutes are dwindling, I tell her I will send her a phone on a contract so we can keep connected, and I'll look into how to get her healthcare and find work near me. I'm in emergency mode now, figuring how this can work. All I can think about is Cheryl out on the streets and sick. I am wondering if she is using, and I make myself ask.

"That life is all behind me, I promise," she says. "I just can't seem to make it here."

With Cheryl now in a hotel with at least two meals a day, I find a decent smartphone and FedEx it to her at the hotel. At least now I can talk to her and text without the monthly restriction of minutes.

I tell Cheryl to get to a doctor, and she goes to an urgent care center.

"The doctor told me I have the bug that's going around, to get some cough medicine and stay hydrated. I just don't have any money."

Still skeptical, I hesitate with this next step, quieting the alarm bells ringing in my head.

"Can I send you a pre-paid card for Walgreen's so you can get the things you need there?"

"That would be great."

I go to my local Walgreen's but find out it's nearly impossible to buy her a card in Connecticut to be used immediately in Louisville.

She has an idea. I can deposit a check to her already existing pre-paid credit card, using her passcode. I'm pretty amazed this is possible, and how quickly she figured it out, but I deposit $50 on her card. There seems to be no better solution other than sending a wire transfer at high cost. We can't use Paypal because she doesn't have a bank account.

"This should get you through the week," I tell her. "Since you have a room and two meals a day, use the money just to get medicine and juices right now." She agrees.

I feel somewhat in control since I have access to her account using her passcode. She thanks me again and again, and I watch the charges come through from Walgreen's. The cold medicine alone puts a big dent in the $50.

"I found a guide for shelters and other help in Louisville. If I send you a pdf, can you see it on the phone, or at the library?" Now that she has a smartphone, I can send her links.

The guide shows the shelters she couldn't get into, and I learn the number of beds for women is far less than for men. There are drug rehabilitation centers in the city, and I ask Cheryl again, "Should we look at that option?"

No, she tells me. "All I need is to get back on my feet."

I call the local Jewish Family Services and explain I need to find a place for my niece to stay, and help finding employment. The counselor there says they can help, and for Cheryl to make an appointment. Although they are on vacation next week, they can leave her a Kroger's grocery card to get food right away.

"They are pretty far from me," Cheryl says. "I don't have a bus pass or money for the fare."

The Louisville MTA office is just a few blocks from her hotel, and I prepay a bus pass that she can pick up there. This will help her to be more mobile in looking for work too.

It is the week before Christmas, and there are no beds available in any of the shelters. Jewish Family Services has no immediate options.

Cheryl has a doctor appointment and an MRI scheduled to look at her back pain—which takes up two days. She also gets into the mental health clinic to see about her anti-depressants. It feels like these are necessary steps to stabilize her situation. I put another $50 on her pre-paid card and pray I am doing the right thing.

In the meantime, I tell her I'm calling her father. She sighs, but I insist. They haven't talked in many months. I feel her father should know the situation, and I also hope he can help. We have been in touch sporadically this past year. I often felt Phil had been unfairly vilified over the years since his divorce from my sister, but a measure of loyalty to her kept me at arm's length. We had kept an amicable, if distant, relationship, which at least allows me to contact him in an emergency like this. The last time I reached out to him was as Cheryl was being released from prison and she needed him to get her birth certificate in order to obtain health care. When we talk this time, he is understandably hesitant, but says he'll help. I remind myself he has been through very tough times with Cheryl.

"He's paying to keep you in the hotel through next week," I tell Cheryl briskly. "Please text him and thank him." I give her his number.

That week I check her account and see she has charged one small item at Walgreen's, and then taken $40 in cash from an ATM against the pre-paid card.

I am alarmed at this and talk to my husband about it before I overreact and think the worst. We decide it is not overreacting to question her about why she would do this.

"The machine at Walgreen's wasn't working, so I went down the street and used the card at the ATM. I don't want you to worry—really—it was for the medicine for my eyes."

She texts me a horrible picture of her swollen eyes from an infection. This is plausible, and even as I envision how many small plasticine bags of heroin might be purchased with my $40, I let it go.

Christmas Eve this year is also the first night of Hanukkah, and I text her a photo of my grandmother's menorah with the first candle.

Can you send me a picture every night of Hanukkah? she texts back. Just reading her request brings tears.

And, of course, I do. One with her cousin, my boy Justin, smiling broadly behind the menorah.

We talk about the possibility of her coming up to me in Connecticut, and I give her the name of surrounding towns where she can start looking at opportunities for work and housing. She writes them down. I'm starting my own search, going to businesses near me to see if they will consider hiring a person with a felony on her record, with my recommendation. I am not having much luck with retailers and restaurants, or even a warehouse nearby.

Housing is another difficult issue, since I live in one of the most expensive states in the country. David and I discuss having Cheryl stay with us for a while, at least at first, which is probably the only solution. As I envision this, I realize I don't fully trust my niece. The stories of her stealing from her mother and grandmother still linger as I think about leaving her alone in our house when I must travel. Friends who have experience with recovering addicts tell me not to have her live with me. *You will upend your whole life.*

Then I discover how difficult it will be to keep her health insurance when she leaves Kentucky. She has several health concerns and needs coverage. Even as I feel guilty, and that a stronger person could figure this all out, I tell Cheryl it's too complicated to bring her here, and I'll help her find her way where she is right now. Maybe at a later time we can talk about a move.

She doesn't argue, just a low mutter, "I know. I understand."

On Christmas day, we talk in the morning, and she tells me she is going to see a holiday display with a friend she met at the Salvation Army. She sounds almost happy. I tell her to have a good time.

On Monday, I urge her to make an appointment with the counselor at Jewish Family Services, and she does. I know this because I am in touch with the counselor, which I let Cheryl know. We also talk about getting temporary day work, as she has done in the past. They have to be at the sign-in location by 6 a.m. and wait to see if they get assigned. On Wednesday, she manages to get some hours of work. She makes around $20.

Although we talk twice each day, I feel like the urgency to find her a job is mostly on my end. I'm sending her leads and giving her advice about restaurants and hotels that are hiring. When she says she's followed up, I keep thinking about what I believe I would do in this situation—though I have never been in anything close—which is to knock on every door in the city until someone hired me for something.

Finally, on December 30, she gets a bed at the Salvation Army. I know she isn't happy about being at the shelter, but both her dad and I agreed she has to be responsible for herself in some way. We can't keep her in a hotel indefinitely. I also learned she can't return to Florida, where her father and sister live, because of an outstanding warrant.

The following week is taken up with follow-up doctor appointments, a mandatory TB test to be able to stay at the Salvation Army, and signing up for housing benefits.

"I have to have three people verify I am homeless and need the help."

She has three of her homeless friends sign notes verifying she is homeless. This seems like the most ridiculous thing I have heard yet.

Knowing I am scheduled to leave the next week for a conference, I quell my misgivings and deposit another $50 in Cheryl's pre-paid card account.

I check with the Jewish Family Services counselor to see if Cheryl showed up for her appointment, and they tell me she did.

"Can you help her?"

"We did an assessment, and we will set her up with a job placement counselor. We still don't have any housing options right now."

Although the counselor is pleasant, she doesn't seem concerned about the urgency of someone without a place to live, with no means of income. I remind myself that Cheryl is only one person among many clients who need help.

Cheryl also has an appointment with the Salvation Army counselor the next day. I hope one of these people can do something more than set up another appointment. It seems like every step takes three times as long as it should.

By the time I leave for my weeklong conference in Key West, I feel like Cheryl has a blueprint for her days of job and housing searches. I know she has a warm bed at the Salvation Army, and at least one hot meal a day.

"I can still text and talk to you while I'm gone," I tell her.

I check her account one more time and see that again she has taken $40 in cash from the same ATM.

"Walgreen's machine is still down," she tells me. "Don't worry, Aunt Judy, I'm not doing anything I shouldn't with the money."

BREATHE

WE'RE WATCHING THE MASSIVE WOMEN'S MARCH protest in Washington, D.C. on our small kitchen TV, making some dinner and pouring wine. Seeing the public outrage brings me a measure of hope. I've only been back from Florida for a day and am still adjusting to the cold Connecticut January. Having just been with a community of writers magnified for me the danger of Trump. I'm furious that some of my writer colleagues are justifiably worried their families may be deported under the new regime. The election was a shock, leaving many of us feeling like we are players in a horror film with no script.

Cheryl had been relegated to the back of my mind during the conference. I had only texted with her once all week, whereas before I had been texting and calling twice a day. In our last text she'd told me she had three interviews for jobs scheduled in the coming week. She asked about my conference, about my travel plans, how I was feeling. I felt she was moving forward toward some stability and allowed myself to relax.

Placing my wine glass carefully on the counter before fumbling for my ringing phone in my pocket, I see the "unknown caller" ID and am pretty sure they have the wrong number. Until I hear my name, asking if I am Cheryl's aunt.

David shoots me a questioning look, but I turn away toward the wall to focus on the words coming at me.

What is it about hearing something you don't want to hear, that does not make sense to you, that animates your hands to fly to your face, your head, your heart? I can't keep my arms and hands still as I try to understand the words this doctor in Louisville is saying. My palms spring to the top of my head. To keep the news from penetrating my brain? I lean on the counter, because I am afraid I will fall. This works for a few seconds until the doctor realizes I have not responded and repeats what he has already told me twice. Something about a heart infection. Found unresponsive. Bleeding out. Did everything possible. No, there is no time to get here. To be with her, at least that. To hold her hand. Nothing more to do. What? What? There must be something! My ears must be blocked, my hearing compromised. I ask again, "If I get on a plane within the hour?" I cradle the phone closer with both hands to be sure I am hearing this right, the words still incomprehensible.

My feeling of déja vu is overwhelming—reliving the call from the oncologist in Florida about my sister, Cheryl's mother. "What do you mean it's not working? You said it would shrink it! Try something else—a different drug—you can't just give up!" I kept him on the phone arguing for five minutes as he repeated, "I'm sorry, I know this is hard to hear. Those were the strongest drugs we have. There is nothing else to try." I thought, *this can't be happening. This cannot be the way my indestructible sister dies. Not my sister who survived a plane crashing into her kitchen and nearly incinerating her into ash!*

Cheryl had grasped my arm when Linda went into cardiac arrest as a nurse cleaned her breathing tube. Something had come loose and caught in her throat. Her worst nightmare, Linda had told me, was not being able to breathe. Was that a premonition? Or a subconscious memory from her two-year-old self; hot smoke curling into her lungs before she lost consciousness? Cheryl looked to me at that moment—to do something—I think she still believed I could. But I had no way to fix this. We stood together, huddled in the corner of the room while the doctors and nurses tried to resuscitate her mother. I have never felt so helpless.

Until now.

The ER doctor explains, for the third time, what he feels I should do. Is he supposed to do this? Tell me she should die? That she most probably is brain dead, and it will be kinder to let her go?

Breathe. You have been holding your breath.

"Can you give permission for the DNR?"

I do not respond.

Breathe.

"I need a family member's permission. Her boyfriend gave your number as next of kin."

Breathe.

He repeats, "Are you able to give permission to let her go?"

Breathe.

"No."

Although I have taken responsibility until now, I can't do it for this final decision. I tell the doctor there is a sister, there is a father. Apparently, I am gathering brain cells to function again, for the actions needed. The calls to Debbie and Phil are nearly the same as the one I endured with the doctor—though I give them his number and him theirs, so they can speak directly. Debbie and her father don't speak to each other, so I become their mediator even now.

There is a muddled decision by either Debbie or Phil—I don't know which—to approve the Do Not Resuscitate order.

I glance at the Yahrzeit candle on my kitchen table and realize today's date—January 21—one day before the plane crashed into our house in 1952. Just an hour from now, it will be the exact date. People tell me this is a coincidence, but I don't believe that anymore. Not after Linda died exactly on Donna's birthday.

The last phone call I receive from the hospital in Louisville is short. Though I had seen the tidal wave coming, hearing that Cheryl is dead thrusts me under the depths. Before I can catch my breath, the nurse says her boyfriend is there and wants to speak to me. How is he even there? I had not heard his name from Cheryl in many months. What did he have to do with this worst possible end? Before I can protest, he is on the phone.

"Aunt Judy, (*Aunt Judy!*) I can't believe she is gone. I loved her so much, I truly did. I held her hand as she left this world. I can't believe it. She loved you so much. I asked if I could be admitted to the mental health unit tonight. I need help. I am devastated."

Instead of asking all the questions his presence brings up, I tell him I am grateful she was not alone, and I mean it. That someone who cared for her was with her in the end. He is in trouble too, I understand, though I have no energy for him right now.

Unbelievably, I have to consult with Phil and Debbie separately about what should be done with Cheryl's body. We can't just leave her in Kentucky, I say to each. In several individual conversations, we agree on cremation and a memorial service in Florida, where Cheryl grew up. Phil says he will arrange for the cremation, the shipping of the ashes, pay for the memorial service. Debbie will organize the service.

"She would want a rabbi, let me handle that," I tell them.

As Cheryl's death becomes a reality, guilt backs me into a corner and interrogates me. Was I an enabler? Believing her when she told me she was clean? Wishfully thinking she just needed some help getting back on her feet? Slinking away, once again, from asking the hard questions.

A week later, David, Justin, and I are at the Hartford airport, leaving for Cheryl's memorial service when we notice a sizable protest. Although the frightening political news had receded somewhat, even as quick executive orders strip away freedoms, it's the travel ban aimed at Muslims that has mobilized outrage. Telling David we'll meet him at the gate, Justin and I exchange a look of recognition, grab hands and join the protesters. The pain in my throat from screaming feels good and right and necessary, stretching my voice to admonish injustice, to rail at the unfathomable and the incomprehensible. All my current anguish melds into one boiling cauldron, pushing at the confines of my chest until I am crying and screaming and pumping my fists with the crowd. A woman around my age with graying hair gives me a homemade protest sign to wave: *We are all immigrants! No Ban, No Wall, No Trump!* I hold the sign high, grab my son's arm by the elbow—*please God don't let me lose him in the crowd today.* He looks back at me, sees my tears and puts an arm around me as we push back against a world gone mad.

PART *TWO*

CAMUS BE DAMNED

I T's THE LIGHT.

That's why I live in Connecticut. Especially the glow of reds and golds as the sun dips on a fall evening. Golden hour, or magic hour as photographers call it. The perfect time of day to capture a picture. Connecticut's fiery patina at day's end mesmerized me when I came here for college. And never left. Oh sure, there was the boyfriend, then the marriage that kept me here. But somehow those details seem ancillary now. It was the light. It makes you believe winter may never arrive. A delusion that the pleasant moderations of spring, summer and fall will not descend into the dark gray winter.

I am a sucker for this kind of deceit.

The scientific explanation for the ethereal light is that the position of the sun changes with the season, and the angle of the sun falls differently in different latitudes. The sunset sky in New Jersey where I grew up is nothing like here in Connecticut, where I've lived now for over 45 years.

Last fall was particularly beautiful, and I took many pictures of the bright orange and yellow trees. It was a busy time, with a trip to Italy for a writing retreat I co-led, and a biking trip to Vermont with David. My iPhone is filled with the Tuscany hills, smiling faces of writers hoisting wine glasses and traipsing through vineyards, and then the quieter times with my husband in the differently shaped hills of Vermont. I was bolstered in September and October of 2016 by the almost certain knowledge, assured by the polls, that we would usher in our first woman president.

It seemed Cheryl was doing well too. Working full-time for the first time since she'd been out of jail.

I believed in these signs, in the bright autumn "when every leaf is a flower," as Camus wrote. Forgetting, as I did every fall, that leaves die and are crushed under foot, swept aside or burned, and trees stripped bare.

EACH FAMILY IS DYSFUNCTIONAL IN ITS OWN WAY

THE CHAPEL IS A NONDESCRIPT, non-denominational, bland box of a room. When I arrive, I am led into a small consultation room and brought a box of Cheryl's effects that were sent along with her ashes. I steady myself as I lift out the worn jeans, the faded sweater, and tee shirt—all sheared into pieces in the emergency room. In her gold buckled purse are pill bottles, cigarettes, lighter, and a hotel size shampoo bottle that reeks of urine. Leaving all that, I grab the journal that I recognize as the one I'd sent her in jail.

"I want to talk to the rabbi alone," Debbie announces as she enters the room.

"Okay, not a problem." I want this day to be peaceful. Debbie has been curt to me since we arrived.

I leave them together and go back to the chapel.

As the pews fill up, it begins to look almost like a segregated orthodox Jewish funeral, but this congregation is split by loyalties, not gender. Debbie has stationed herself at the door, ushering her friends to her side of the chapel where her husband is holding seats for her and her two sons, making sure her father and his wife are alone on the other side of the room. David and I walk over and assure Phil that we will sit with them. He'd asked me to please do so yesterday, anticipating Debbie's shunning. Debbie gives me a steely look when she sees I am sitting with her father. She is nursing her long-held grievances about his absenteeism in her childhood and what she considers a lack of financial and emotional support. Lately, she blames him for not sending Cheryl to the right rehab. I am beginning to see how removed she is, still, from the true facts. This only adds to my sadness.

We watch the video I made of Cheryl at different ages, with photos sent to me by both Debbie and her father. I did not include the last picture of her, with her weary eyes and her emaciated boyfriend, sent from her cell phone. It is that photo I can't get out of my head.

Who took it the day before she died?

The rabbi, almost a caricature with a white beard and rheumy eyes, ambles up to the podium with his walker. He places it to the side, grabs on to the podium for support and gestures for me to come forward. I understand he wants to say the traditional prayer with the family and perform the ceremony of tearing the Kriah—the black ribbon torn and pinned to mourners to represent the ancient tradition of tearing one's clothes in expression of grief and anger over the loss of a loved one. Debbie is avoiding my gaze as her father joins me to create the family circle with the rabbi. I break away and grab Debbie by the shoulders, surprising myself at my force.

"This, you have to do."

She nods but makes no eye contact and joins the circle. Incredibly, we join hands, the blessing is said, the Kriah pinned and Debbie retreats to her seat. Opposing teams shaking hands before the big game.

Ironically, Debbie was the child who looked most like me. She even had my name as her middle name. As a baby, people often thought she was mine when Linda and I would go out with her girls. She was a sweet, happy kid who loved me with abandon, as I did her. And still do.

The moment we both remember best was at the Jersey shore. We had the usual configuration of blankets and towels around a cooler of bologna sandwiches, chips, and sodas. As soon as we got set up, Debbie and Cheryl grabbed my hand and rushed us into the ocean.

We jumped the waves together and I lifted four-year-old Debbie over the swells. At one point, a big wave caught her and pulled her under, and I lost sight of her in the foam. In a panic, I dove under and scooped her up as she cried, gasped for air and rubbed her eyes.

I wish I knew how to rescue her now.

Justin drifts back and forth between the sides of the room and then settles on sitting with Debbie. I give him no guff about it. He never wants to hurt anyone, and he decided who needed him most right now.

"She just lost her sister," he says as he heads to his seat. How is it that our children seem to surpass us in every way? My boy certainly eclipses me in his compassion, his profession as a social worker just an outgrowth of his innate empathy.

This morning I had broached the subject of transgenerational trauma with Justin as we walked the beach, a light drizzle dampening the sand. We talked about the stress, pain and disappointment in Linda's life and the likely trickle-down trauma to her girls. The link to depression and addiction.

"It's you too, you know," I gently suggest. "You are part of this family too." I only want his awareness, much as I want him to be cognizant of the alcoholism permeating his father's family.

"I'm fine mom, really, don't worry," he said, reaching over to put an arm around my shoulders.

Looking around the room during the memorial service, I know my mother would have had a lot to say about people showing up dressed in shorts and tee shirts. It's Florida, I realize, but not a barbecue, for fuck-sake. The only ones in ties are Phil, David, Justin, and bless his heart, Debbie's older son, who wears a dark suit. I hug him for a long moment in appreciation of this show of respect.

During the brief service the rabbi claims, "We don't know why she died, it's a mystery." The true mystery is why she became addicted in the first place, and why she relapsed. Debbie gets up to talk about her sister—her "best friend who I will miss forever." As she talks, I remember them at ages two and three running and laughing together. Despite her misplaced anger, Debbie's genuine pain at losing her sister fills the room. I want so much to comfort her.

When it's my turn to speak, I surprise myself by making it through the words I've written in Cheryl's memory. The tears fall, but my voice remains stronger than I feel. I want to remember her as the girl who cooked for her grandparents, who stood by me at her mother's deathbed, who wanted to see the Hanukkah lights one more time. The one who held her little sister's hand as they roller-skated down a steep hill. I am trying to obliterate the last few terrible years of her short life, much as I imagine she would want me to.

After the ceremony, Debbie approaches me, looking everywhere but my eyes.

"I'd like her ashes," she points toward the plain steel urn at the front of the chapel, next to the only flowers. It dawns on me Debbie will be the one taking home the arrangement I ordered.

"Of course," I say.

"Can you get them for me?" She gestures toward her father, still at the front of the chapel, and I understand she does not want to pass him to retrieve the urn.

"Really?"

"Please."

After I deliver the urn, Debbie turns away from me and walks outside where her friends are about to release a bunch of balloons in honor of Cheryl. Maybe I should have let her just have a balloon service.

"We would like to take your family to lunch," I say to her back as she watches white balloons drift up into a gray sky.

"Who is going?"

"Just you guys."

"I won't go with him."

"They have to get on the road for the four-hour ride home anyway."

"Okay then."

We take them to our favorite deli in West Palm. We sit at a long table, and Debbie and her husband sit at the farthest end from me.

They do not say a word to me for the entire meal. Her boys, though, tell me about college plans and football games. Prior to this day, I was the beloved aunt, and I can see they are confused by my new status.

We mention we have four hours to kill before our flight home, but there is no offer to come back to their house. When the check arrives, Debbie and her husband immediately go outside to smoke a cigarette. We pay the check and leave. They mumble a thank you for lunch, Debbie still unable to make eye contact, and we go our separate ways. It has started to rain, and we have no umbrella.

CHERYL'S FACEBOOK POST

Cheryl   •••
July 25, 2016 1:05PM

Candle is lit, praying and fasting in memory of
my mom today (7/25/09). . . love you mom,
even if I didn't always show it, always have
and always will. I know you are with me every
day.

So lucky to have had you as my mom.

👍 Like   ↪ Share

*Five months before Cheryl's death, on her mother's yahrzeit day
(day of her death).*

HER CELL PHONE

A WEEK AFTER CHERYL'S MEMORIAL SERVICE, I turn on her cell phone. The one I sent her which the hospital sent back to me. My connection to her then and now.

It's dead, of course, and takes a moment to start up after I plug in a charging cable. It works differently than my iPhone, but the green Message icon at the bottom is the same. I hesitate before clicking it, worried about what I may find.

I scroll through the 502 messages between the two of us, from the time she got this phone until her death a month later. Her messages are upbeat, telling of appointments with counselors, finding a bed in a shelter, looking for work. She writes that she has scheduled an MRI for back pain and set up a visit to a mental health clinic. We even joke in one text about her factory job being like Lucy keeping up with the conveyor belt in the chocolate factory. I remember the phone calls in between texts. Her steady voice. Her laugh. Sounding like the girl I knew. Why didn't I probe more then? Make her more accountable? I am starting to understand my pattern of avoidance. Facing the truth of her continued drug use would have demanded I do something about it.

I see the eight photos I sent of our menorah candles lit for each day of Hanukkah, Justin smiling in one and her text back, "Hi Justin! Great pic!"

Reading my own texts to her is odd.

Have you done this and gone there? Have you called this person I suggested? Looked at this job website? What's up today?—a frequent good morning text.

Or: **Tomorrow is a new beginning! Call me after your appointment.**

I sound like a nag, and eerily chipper. Is that how I sounded to her? Could I have been less annoying? And would that have made any difference? I had thought I was being vigilant, but I see now it wasn't nearly enough.

I find the selfie of her with a terrible eye infection. We discuss getting to a doctor. There's a photo of the room where she slept at the Salvation Army.

It's good to know where you are, and you are warm and have food.

The temperature had dipped to nine degrees there. A certifiable White Flag day. I notice I had not given her a chance to tell me about the bad parts of life in the shelter.

I see the text where she asked me to put money on her cash card and how to execute the transaction. She was very savvy at it.

I just need some cough medicine and some Gatorade to hydrate.

She had a bad cold, probably from sleeping in the house with no heat for weeks, and of course, I complied. She seemed to be trying so hard to get back on her feet.

Text messages from her sister are filled with concern, and they soften my view of Debbie. It was she, after all, who called me when Cheryl needed help. I see their exchange about Hanukkah, and Debbie says she can't find her menorah. Cheryl suggests:

Cover some cardboard with tin foil, and drip wax to hold the candles.

Debbie has advice for Cheryl too.

Apply for unemployment, get your tax refund, rent out the rooms in the abandoned house.

She texts Cheryl news of how her own life was recently upended with the loss of her job. She was finally settling in with her two boys and husband in a new apartment, after sleeping at a friend's for three months. I didn't know any of this. Debbie doesn't ask her sister about drugs or rehab in any of the texts.

After Cheryl met with Jewish Family Services, she texted me:

They def can help me with work clothes, finding work and housing.

She called about some job ads, but said they turned out to be scams.

I texted her a link to a Starbucks help wanted ad, telling her they have good benefits. No response.

Her phone is about to die, she says, and she can't text or call—but just a short time later I see she texted someone about meeting at White Castle.

Then there are texts to numbers I don't recognize. Many notes like:

how long u think?

u still comin?

I'm at MacDonald's

I'm at White Castle

I can come to u, where u at?

Is your dude comin?

Well, that could be anything, I tell myself. But by now I am able to recognize my denial.

I stop when I see,

It's James, U ok momma?

Cheryl had said she wasn't with him anymore and he had gone back to his family in Ohio. She knew I blamed him for much of her trouble and would be unsympathetic if I knew she was back with him. But the date on that message is December 17, so he was there from the beginning of this month-long final chapter.

Then:

How do I know it's good?

Oh it's good.

Just to tell you that you are hot with the cops, they know your name.

And a spat with someone:

I got loyal junkies I takes care of and U r nt 1. Don call wen u sick! This is brown sugar, you gotta taste your shit before you buy.

Let us know when you get different stuff, people are complainin about it.

We're trying to get you more business out here.

I feel the hope drain from me.

When I go through the painstaking task of charting out the messages, lining up the dates and times of calls on a spreadsheet, I realize even as she was texting me about job interviews, looking for housing, getting treatment for her back pain, talking to a disability lawyer—she was meeting drug dealers at McDonald's, or White Castle, or on the street. I check the dates when I deposited money, and the amounts, and sure enough, they coincide with these meetings. I see my texts questioning why she used $40 cash in two days, and her explanations, which in hindsight are thin.

> **I still have $15, woke up sick, Walgreen's machine was still broken to use the debit card. I could use a little help, I really need cough drops, can't stop coughing.**

I am an idiot. I wanted so much to believe her. I had forgotten the warnings from friends: *Addicts lie like it is breathing.*

The messages start December 17, 2016, when the phone was activated, and end January 21, 2017, the day she died, one day short of the anniversary of the plane crash that changed all our lives, with a last text to James at 9:04 am:

> **It's Cheryl, pick up.**

ILLUSIONS

How strange when an illusion dies. It's as though you've lost a child.

— JUDY GARLAND

Illusion: The act of deceiving; the state of being intellectually deceived or misled, something that deceives or misleads intellectually, perception of something objectively existing in such a way as to cause misinterpretation of its actual nature; hallucination.
The Merriam-Webster Dictionary

Meetings are not for me, drugs are in my past and I will never go back to that life.

The word comes from the Middle English, illusioun, from old French, and from the Late Latin illūsiō, illūsiōn-, from Latin, a mocking, irony, from illūsus, past participle of illūdere, to mock.

The Oxford Dictionary

I have two job interviews this week. I used the money for cough medicine.

Illusion is an erroneous perception of reality; an erroneous concept or belief; a false perception.

The Free Dictionary

There was no plane crash.

No dead sister.

Linda is completely normal.

I feel no guilt.

I am fine.

I can save her.

THE MEDICAL REPORT

Okay, just sit, just hold your knees tight. Okay, rock . . .
Oh, God, oh my God . . . Okay, okay . . . somebody's
coming. It'll be okay . . . Just hold yourself, hold yourself
. . . it's gonna be okay . . . Somebody's coming.

— CARRIE FISHER,
Postcards from the Edge

CHERYL'S FATHER HELPED ME OBTAIN HER MEDICAL REPORT from the University of Louisville Hospital, even though he doesn't want to know the details. Why do I? Why does dissecting the minutiae of her last days on this earth seem so necessary?

Maybe it's a way of not abandoning her to die alone on the park bench.

The report is 463 pages, and I wade through it for weeks, looking up medical terms and drug definitions. I send sections to a nurse I know and to a medical student who has agreed to help me decipher it.

The Emergency Medical Service (EMS) report has no record of administering Narcan (naloxone) when they found Cheryl. I call the Louisville EMS and talk to the head paramedic, lying that I am writing an article about how Narcan is administered. He tells me they ALWAYS administer Narcan.

"We almost use it as a diagnostic tool." Even if the person is in cardiac arrest? I ask. "Yes, even then."

She was intubated in the ambulance and put on a ventilator at the hospital. It was determined she had suffered cardiac arrest, was in respiratory failure. Her brain had been deprived of oxygen for an unspecified amount of time. She sustained brain damage, but the report does not say exactly when. Was it in Cherokee Park? Was it in the ambulance? Or later, in the hospital? What was she aware of when?

Here are salient details from the ER report, my notes in italics. Writing these down is the closest I will get to being there with her.

EVENT DATE/TIME: 1/21/2017 16:00 EST

The time note is disturbing, given the last text she sent her boyfriend was at 9:03 am, seven hours earlier.

DESCRIPTION OF EVENT:

1600 - PATIENT ARRIVES FROM ER WITH RN :BD. OOZING BLOODY HEMATOMAS ON LEFT SHOULDER AND RIGHT FEMORAL NOTED.

How did these happen? Did someone grab her?

BLOODY SECRETIONS FROM ABDOMEN

BLEEDING FROM IC *(injection)* AND OLD PIV *(peripheral intravenous)* SITE

PATIENT IS IN DIC *(disseminated intravascular coagulation, bleeding out)*

PATIENT ON LEVOPHED *(norepinephrine, to bring up her blood pressure)*

1L EMERGENT BOLUS *(emergency medicine bundle)* ORDERED AT THIS TIME AND ADMINISTERED PER MD ORDERS. 1615- PT SBP <40.

1730- EMERGENT FFP *(fresh, frozen plasma)* AND CRYO *(cryoprecipitate for bleeding)* INFUSIONS STARTED EMERGENTLY

ARTIC SUN *(a non-invasive patient temperature management system)* STARTED EMERGENTLY

DR. __ REPORTS THAT HE HAS SPOKEN TO PATIENT AUNT (JUDY) AND REPORTS THAT JUDY HAS SPOKEN TO PATIENT SISTER (NEXT OF KIN). DR. ___ REQUESTS RN TO SPEAK WITH JUDY TO CONFIRM THAT FAMILY WISHES ARE FOR DNR WITH FULL TREATMENT. DURING CONVERSATION, JUDY ASKS IF ANYONE HAS SPOKEN TO PATIENT'S FATHER. RN RECORDS PATIENT FATHER'S NUMBER.

JUDY CONFIRMS THAT HER AND SISTER WISH FOR DNR

WITH FULL TREATMENT.

DR. ___ REPORTS THAT HE WILL CONTINUE TO CONTACT FATHER AND SISTER TO OBTAIN OFFICIAL CODE STATUS.

She was given a transfusion of the blood type we shared, A positive.

She was unresponsive, the record says. Still, the recommendation reads: **BEDREST.**

Hepatitis C is listed under infectious disease information, and also polycythemia, which produces excess blood cells. Was this condition why there was so much blood?

The toxicology report specified heroin, methamphetamines, and oxycodone.

Some drugs linger in the body longer than others. Oxycodone, for example, can last from one to two days, and meth between eight and 24 hours, while heroin may be flushed out anywhere from three minutes to an hour. It all depends on how much is taken and the person's liver and kidney function and metabolism. So, it's possible she had taken the oxy a couple of days before the incident, the meth the day before, and the heroin a moment before. There is no record of paraphernalia found near her. My gut tells me her boyfriend would have cleaned that up before the ambulance arrived.

I am confused as to why they gave her Fentanyl, the lethal synthetic opioid that may well have also been mixed with the fatal dose of drugs. Medical professionals tell me Fentanyl is only given for pain. They agree it is unlikely Cheryl was in pain at that point, since brain function was non-existent. Nevertheless, the report states the reason for the Fentanyl is for **PAIN INTENSITY**. The only explanation may be they didn't know for sure what kind of pain she was in, so toward the end, they gave her the Fentanyl as a measure of comfort, which I choose to believe. They also gave her Lorazepam (Ativan) for anxiety. Why?

They did an ultrasound of her heart's superior vena cava, which revealed an irregularity. During the first call I received, the doctor only said Cheryl had an infection in her heart called endocarditis. What role did that infection play in her death?

AT 21:57 EST ON 1/21/2017: PATIENT TERMINALLY EX-TUBATED AT FAMILY REQUEST.

PATIENT'S S/O (SIGNIFICANT OTHER) WAS PRESENT AND TEARFUL. HE ADDRESSED STORIES ABOUT THEIR RELATIONSHIP AND HIS GRIEF. SAID HE WAS EXPECT-ING ARRIVAL OF PATIENT'S FAMILY. HE SAID HE WOULD NEED SOME "EXTRA SUPPORT" IF SHE PASSES AWAY. THE CHAPLAIN OFFERED AN EMPATHETIC EAR AND PRAYER.

TIME OF DEATH: 22:12 EST, 1/21/2017.

CHERYL'S FACEBOOK POST

Cheryl
July 26, 2016 5:41PM

When they thought you'd never get clean
BUT THEN U DID!

👍 Like   ➤ Share

Five months before her death.

LOUISVILLE, LOUISVILLE, LOUISVILLE

I**T'S LIKE STEPPING ON A NAIL IN THE GRASS** when I read newspaper reports of how the opioid epidemic is especially rampant in Louisville, Kentucky. I learn Cheryl's overdose may have been part of a rash of deaths linked to a batch of heroin laced with the deadly drug Fentanyl.

Six months after her death, I read an article in *The New York Times* about a breakthrough rehabilitation program in a Kentucky prison. GED classes, 12-Step meetings, corrective thinking instruction, meditation, and counseling. I wonder if she missed this kind of program by a matter of months. The article describes a supportive atmosphere of recovery; inmates becoming a kind of family. They look out for one another and support each other, like a 12-Step program. Kentucky has a dozen of these programs now for the multitudes of incarcerated opiate addicts.

Would a program like this one have saved my niece from becoming one of the 64,000 overdose deaths that year? I try to feel encouraged by the progress for treatment in prisons.

Now, a new Republican healthcare bill threatens to throw 22 million people off the Affordable Care Act healthcare insurance. Medicaid and Medicare will be drastically cut. Humana Healthcare is pulling out of the market in Kentucky.

Cheryl would have been left with no healthcare insurance and no treatment for her depression, Hep C or polycythemia.

NOT NEWS

I SCAN THE ONLINE ARCHIVES of the *Courier-Journal of Louisville* for the week of January 21, 2017, looking for any mention of Cheryl's death in the paper. I find stories of the opioid epidemic in the city and neighboring areas, lots of overdose statistics, but no mention of finding her in Cherokee Park. No notice of her death.

Her death did not warrant even one line.

The first draft of the obituary I write for local papers where Cheryl's father and sister live includes the cause of death as overdose. When Debbie objects, I omit the actual cause and just include a suggested donation to a national addiction recovery foundation. Debbie nixes that too.

"They'll know it was drugs if we do that."

The obit is a testament to our collaborative dishonesty. Upholding the illusion, even in death.

HER JOURNAL

IT TAKES ME TWO MONTHS to open Cheryl's journal. I'd sent it to her in jail, hoping that writing down her thoughts would help her understand herself—as writing has done for me. Now I want clues about her life, what happened to her—or some proof this is all a mistake. Slowly, I am closing in on my own denial.

Knowing the end of this story, I start at the back. Here is some of what I find.

Under the heading LIBRARY:

Labor Works Map

Louisville Job Show

Craigslist

Unemployment Office

Hollander (a factory where she once worked).

Lures 4 bass

glands in neck-lymph nodes

Exorcist – orig.girl

WellCare PCPs

Print Fake Mail (?)

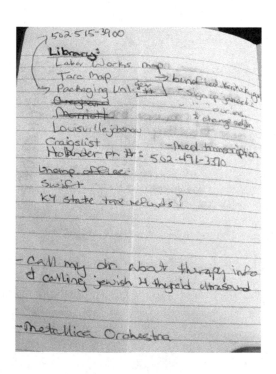

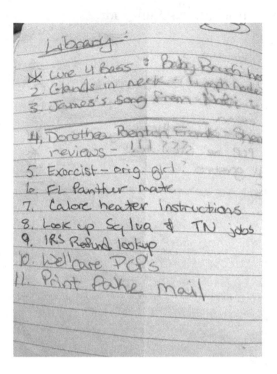

One page has addresses and directions, phone numbers, hours they are open.

Several doctors' names and numbers are noted, with instructions about meds.

A To-Do list:

open gmail account (which I told her to do)

update resume

finish labor ready app online

get new phone

eye exam ("I need glasses Aunt Judy")

chiropractor

call PCP for stool test

Call gastro

F.S. (?)

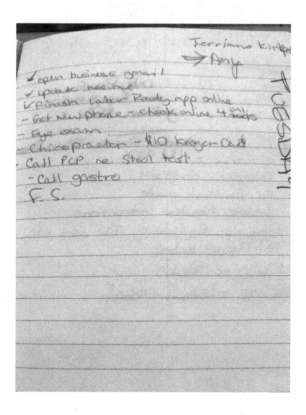

A list of towns near me where she might look for work. This plunges me under a wave of sadness, knowing I had given her this hope of coming to me and then took it away.

Newington

New Britain

Berlin

Wethersfield

Rocky Hill

Expenses are tracked on one page titled FOOD & DRINK.

A list of shelters:

Church basement: Broadway and 31st, 11th & Muhammad Ali

Midwest Church

St. Elizabeth

St. Georges

Salvation Army

For food:

Mobile Pantry

Food Box

BBQ

Food Stamps

Kroger cards

Then there are two pages of phone numbers. Mine at the top. One titled "Mom" has me befuddled. Her mom had been dead for six years. I call the number, but there is no answer and no voice mail set up. Some of the names and numbers are listed twice, and sometimes three times. Her nephew is listed three times with the same number.

Three pages contain passwords, pin numbers and logins with some kind of system to keep the meager funds she collected, and to find benefit systems to help her survive on the street. Obama phone. Paypal, Wellcare, Benefind. Amex Serve, Turbo Tax, EBI,

JPay, Credit Karma. She was trying so very hard.

She must have gotten the eye exam because her eyeglass prescription is here, under which she lists online sources for glasses.

The page for login passwords is dog-eared and decorated with a little illustration of a paper clip, colored in precisely with a little sad face.

The next page is in a handwriting I don't recognize, or maybe hers when impaired, all barely legible: December 5, 3:00 pm. — SS card 4 everyone—Proof of income or none for November, locate form online.

In the middle of 10 blank pages is this in red ink:

Date:_____

_____

2   _____

Nothing else.

Then a page with her prescriptions, prescription numbers, dates for renewals and phone number for Walgreens. Gabapentin, Doxepin, Aspirin, Levothyroxine, Vitamin D3.

I can't figure out what the numbers are next to a list of motels. Some seem like dates, some seem to be rates, then a phone number. A list of restaurants, hotels and the Horseshoe Casino (where she once worked) has dates, addresses and job link URLs.

A hand-drawn map shows the locations of Jewish Hospital and

University of Louisville Hospital, and something named Norton. I look it up and find it is a Primary Care facility.

One page devoted to unemployment claims gives me a window into when she became unemployed. The file date is 4/20/16. First payment 5/6/16. Eligible review 6/1/16.

There was a call with me in May noted under IRELAND:

5/3/16 – talked to Aunt Judy for help.

This was about trying to claim an inheritance James thought he may be entitled to from a relative in Ireland. There is a list of attorneys to call. It sounded far-fetched when she told me about it, and I didn't think they had a chance of getting any money. My advice, which was no help at all, was to find an attorney to help them, which now seems as ludicrous an idea as the possibility of the inheritance itself.

I'm beginning to see Cheryl used the journal like scrap paper, opening to any page to make the note of the day without much of a pattern. Toward the front of the book is a note for an appointment for Feb. 8 at Phoenix Mental Health—an appointment she didn't live to keep. Also, the number for Jewish Family Services, and the address for the pain management doctor she saw just two days before her death.

One page lists:

Methadone Clinic, address and hours

Syringe Exchange, days and hours open.

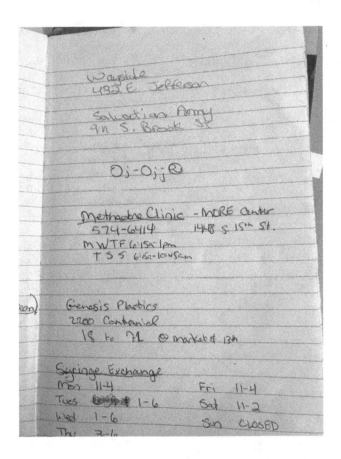

A chart for work hours at the casino begins in January (I assume 2016) and goes through March. Then there is a break in time and two more slots in July.

Her Medicaid number is listed on the first page of the journal—

along with "gastro" doctors, and the name of my sister's third husband, and "Peducah?" Did she plan to look him up? He was the man
who was so depressed that I hardly remember him speaking.

I close the book.

Part of me wants to put the journal in a drawer and never see it
again. It's too much to imagine each day she wrote in it. I see her
huddled in a library, the far corner of a fast-food restaurant, or on a
park bench. The struggle for survival, for money, her battle against
self-destruction is so visceral in these pages. I can feel her striving
for normalcy. Trying to recover her health, hold a job, find a place to
live—interrupted consistently by her addiction.

CHERYL'S FACEBOOK POSTS

Cheryl   •••
October 16, 2015 11:24PM

She says she's fine
But she's going insane.
She says she feels good
But she's in a lot of pain.
She says it's nothing
But it's really a lot.
She says she's okay.
But really she's not.
She puts on a smile
To hide the pain.
But deep in her heart
She's going insane.
#abuse

👍 Like   ↷ Share

Cheryl
November 5, 2015 1:02AM   •••

I thought I was holding up okay until someone
asked me how I was holding up and I just
started crying. No, I guess I'm not okay.

👍 Like   ↪ Share

CHERYL'S MEDS

USING THE LIST OF HER MEDICATIONS IN HER JOURNAL, I look them up online. I'm looking for interactions to explain her bleed out, the infection in her heart, even as I realize the futility of this exercise.

GABAPENTIN is used to prevent and control seizures, relieve nerve pain and as an anticonvulsant. Further reading mentions its use for bipolar disorder. Then, strangely, it lists side effects as depression, suicidal thoughts or other mood problems. Conflicting drugs that can cause drowsiness are alcohol, antihistamines, anxiety drugs and any narcotics.

DOXEPIN

Antidepressant; Tricyclic

ASPIRIN

For her polycythemia blood disease, which produces excess red blood cells. Treatment is phlebotomy, which I doubt she'd had recently.

LEVOTHYROXINE is a thyroid medicine that replaces a hormone normally produced by the thyroid gland to regulate the body's energy and metabolism. It's used when the body does not produce enough of this hormone on its own. These imbalances can be caused by radiation treatment, surgery, or cancer.

VITAMIN D3

WE HAVE NO SECRETS

The past is never where you think you left it.

— KATHERINE ANNE PORTER

THERE IS SO MUCH I DON'T KNOW ABOUT CHERYL.

Did Cheryl and her mother ever talk about their feelings? About Linda's trauma of the plane crash and her subsequent years of recovery and alienation? How a parent's trauma is necessarily the child's? Or about Cheryl's addiction and sexual abuse? As far as I know, her depression was not diagnosed until she found herself in jail at 40 for the crimes associated with her drug use.

One day, not long before Linda died, sitting with Linda and

Cheryl in Cheryl's house in Florida, they were smoking, sharing lighters and cigarettes and laughing about some reminiscence. The easy interaction I often saw between them. Cheryl was playing host, delivering cold drinks to us on the small worn couch, keeping her large lab away from Linda's tiny dog nestled on her lap. My sister shifted uncomfortably on the couch, winced and adjusted her hip. She mentioned she had run out of her pain pills, and Cheryl said not to worry, "I can get some for you." When they saw my shock, they changed the subject quickly. I never asked. I convinced myself everything was fine. Oh, but I was good at this.

When Linda died, I cried with Cheryl and told her how much I would miss my big sister.

"You still have me," she said. "I'm exactly like Mom, so it's almost the same." And we laughed for a minute, even as a sliver of dread cut through me.

One major hole in my narrative is whether Cheryl was ever pregnant. I suspected it from the offhand comment during that one phone conversation from prison. I'm not sure why I am fixated on it.

Her father said he knew of no pregnancy. But, he conceded, "I was out of her life so much, there were lots of things I didn't know." I imagine another sad-eyed girl, lost in some other family, or someday showing up at my door.

When things got rough, my sister left out many details. Only when I was a witness did I get the real story.

One New Year's Eve, I visited Linda and her daughters in New Jersey; Cheryl was maybe five, her sister Debbie four. Linda was recently remarried and, I thought, happy. That's the way it seemed anyway, from my distance in Connecticut. At 25, I was not-so-happily-married, newly separated, and came to spend the holiday with her. I volunteered to stay in with the girls while she and her second husband, Mark, went out to dinner. Even though I had no experience with kids, I loved these girls fiercely and planned a fun evening with hats and blowers and snacks.

The three-hour drive from Connecticut was cold, wet and gray, and I was looking forward to a warm night in with my nieces.

"Aunt Judy!" They greeted me with squeals, swamping me with hugs as I entered the small apartment. My sister laughed when I told her it had taken me three turns around the complex to find her door in the maze of same-same brick buildings.

"You still can't find your way out of a paper bag."

She and Mark were already dressed for their night out. Linda gave the girls a Happy New Year hug, and they were out the door.

We'd had our slices of pizza and were working on ice cream sundaes, spraying more and more whipped cream as we scooped it up, the girls laughing with each new spritz of fluffy cream, when Linda and Mark burst noisily through the front door. I was on the couch facing the kitchen, where their argument began to escalate, and I continued to engage the kids to distract them. But they seemed not at all aware, blithely watching TV, never looking up at their mother as their stepfather yelled abuses. I startled when he called her a bitch and cunt, but when he grabbed Linda's wrists, I made my way to her side. Still, the kids never looked up from their show. How many of these fights had they witnessed?

Mark, a burly construction worker with slicked back black hair, saw he was outnumbered and looked at me in disbelief as I poured his bottle of Wild Turkey down the sink. Something in my eyes warned him off, and he knew not to challenge me, although he was twice my size. He cursed another "Jesus fucking Christ" and stormed out. I put my arm around Linda's shoulders for a moment, and silently, we both began dumping the remaining four liquor bottles down the drain. I looked over at the girls, still eating their ice cream, never looking away from the TV. We never spoke about it again. Now I so wish we had. Maybe it would have helped us both understand the dynamic in our relationship, in our family, in ourselves. Maybe facing this hard truth would have bolstered us all. Perhaps given Cheryl the strength she needed.

Recently, Cheryl's father verified what I had suspected. Mark had later sexually abused Cheryl. Linda had him arrested, which she never told me. All I knew at the time was they got divorced. I have no idea if my parents were in on this secret, but I have to think my sister would have confided in my mother. Despite their arguments, they were very close. For Cheryl, I now believe the abuse opened a fissure of emptiness, the hungry ghost she would try to feed for the rest of her life.

PICTURE THIS

I don't know a soul who's not been battered,
I don't have a friend that feels at ease.
I don't know a dream that's not been shattered,
Or driven to its knees.
But it's all right, it's all right—
For we've lived so well so long.
Still, when I think of the road we're traveling on
I can't help it, I wonder what's gone wrong.

– PAUL SIMON
American Tune

M Y ONLY REMAINING LINK TO CHERYL is her dad, Phil. We've been in touch more since her death, and I think I can say we are friends. Debbie will not speak to me because I sat with him at the memorial service. A couple of weeks ago, Phil sent me a text asking if I wanted to see some family slides of Cheryl and Debbie.

"Yes, of course I want to," was my immediate reply.

"You'll see I spent a lot of time with them when they were young," he writes back. He so badly wants me to know this.

He sends a box packed with seven full Kodak Carousel trays and two large metal slide boxes. A few thousand slides. But without a slide projector, I have no way to look at these. Holding each one up to a light bulb will take forever and won't show me what I am looking for—the child kernel of Cheryl.

A harrowing eBay auction rewards me with a slide projector. I am grateful and amazed it works so well. Hearing the whir of the fan as the spotlight shines on the blank wall brings me back to the days when we viewed slides of grainy seaside and mountain vistas on a machine like this, our friends feigning interest until one of them fell asleep on the couch.

Popping in the first tray, I slog through many landscape shots I have no interest in. Then I notice the notes on the inside of the box. Down a third of the way, I see the girls' names and click my way toward them. In one slide they are perhaps two and three years old, sitting under a tree, smiling with their arms around each other. I recognize the house my sister and Phil bought in New Jersey. Linda and Phil show up in other pictures, looking young and hopeful—and happy. I can't help thinking they had a good start. Will I ever have the courage to ask Phil what happened between them? My sister never gave me much of an answer. What would have been different for them all if they had stayed together and brought these two babies up in that pretty house in the suburbs?

As I think this, I brush away the fantasy. I believe now that my sister was ill equipped from the start, fed with the illusion that she did not suffer any trauma, was not a victim and had nothing to overcome. My parents didn't know how to prepare her or to seek the kind of help she needed growing up.

I continue through the slides to find Cheryl as a two-year-old, a four-year-old, a five-year-old without any change in her cherub-like visage. Her eyes still hold the "spark of mischief" my dad named. In many pictures, her younger sister looks at her with the worship I remember I had for my own big sister. Cheryl often has a protective arm around Debbie's shoulder. The shots of them being goofballs together, dancing and making funny faces, bring back memories of those days when we were all so oblivious of the future—and the shadows of the past.

In slides of Linda holding newborn Cheryl, my sister looks enthralled with her first baby. My parents hold baby Cheryl, unabashedly smitten with their first granddaughter, pure love in their eyes. With this viewing, I am pummeled with three generations of grief. I pause often on a photo to study the face of my father, my mother, my sister.

I think of a line in Joan Didion's book *Blue Nights* when she finds a trove of old photographs: *In fact they serve only to make clear how inadequately I appreciated the moment when it was here.*

There are many baby pictures of Cheryl, and I acknowledge the one who is not pictured—the photographer—Phil. Doting on his first child, amazed as all new parents are, at having produced this little human being. Cheryl smiles for him. Fixates on him, enamored with her daddy while he photographs.

There I am, well the back of my head anyway, as Linda unwraps my first gift to Cheryl. A ridiculously huge doll I made for her, having no experience whatsoever with babies. I remember how I sewed it as I travelled across the country with my soon-to-be husband, waiting in the car while he had appointments. He makes an appearance in one slide too, which startles me.

I ask Phil about one slide that looks like an old friend of my sister's. He tells me, yes, it's Nancy. She was Linda's childhood friend who often came to her rescue when other kids shunned her, made fun of her or were afraid they would catch whatever gave her the scars. Nancy would leave any stickball game if Linda was excluded. Her loyalty to Linda made all the difference to my sister's childhood.

In my head, I calculate Linda and Phil's ages when they had their girls—only in their early 20's. While I am watching this unfolding of their young lives together, I text Phil how sorry I am they couldn't find a way to stay together. To my surprise, he agrees. When he offers to explain what happened, I don't reply. I'm not sure I can betray my sister in this way, when she is not here to defend herself.

Even though it's emotionally draining, and I feel the grief dripping through me, I view all the slides twice, three times, over the course of a week. I study each picture and try to imagine what happened before and after each was taken. Where were they in their story—in the picture at the beach, at the cookout, at the Thanksgiving dinner? What detail am I missing that is just beyond the reach of the camera lens?

In the end, I still haven't found the turning point where Cheryl's unbridled joy morphed into what we called her Mona Lisa smile.

When I'm done, I lean back in my chair and let the fan run so the bulb doesn't burst.

Cheryl, Age 9

Age 14

Age 4

Age 7

Age 9

1983

Age 14

WHO ARE YOU?

**Deception, deception, deception . . .
You live in a dream, you manufacture illusions.**

— Amanda in THE GLASS MENAGERIE
by Tennessee Williams

I CAN'T HELP THINKING that the political climate right now, with truth as elusive as a dream, is connected somehow with my search for the real facts about Cheryl's life and death. For whatever reason, I crave to know the reality of who she was—whom it is I am mourning. To that end, I register online for her criminal background report.

The accessible records go back as far as an arrest in 1998 and end with the one that landed her in jail in 2014 for felony theft.

I had the story in my head that she was *fine for at least 10 years, clean and with a steady job.* I have said this out loud.

Now I discover I'd been deceived in this, too. Right in the middle of the "she's fine" timeline, Cheryl was arrested for prostitution. This was in 2000, the year I married David. I'd invited her to the wedding in Connecticut, but she couldn't make it. No one said why. My sister never told me about this, or any of the other arrests I find on the investigative website. By now, though, this isn't a surprise. Linda curated my version of her life carefully. And I was her best accomplice. What other explanation is there for never looking this up before now?

Our lies to ourselves and each other were symbiotic. Would I have acted differently if I had known these facts?

Cheryl was arrested for possession of drug production paraphernalia just three months after her mother died in 2009. It dawns on me that Linda knew about the weed growing operation, even as she confronted recovery from lung cancer, when I suggested she stay with Cheryl during chemo treatments and she objected so strongly. Linda wrote on the pad by her bed—because she was intubated—"not with that big dog"—and didn't tell me the real reason. This was our pattern, I realize more and more, to protect me from the ugly and horrifying truth. Much as my parents did. Never talking about the dead sister, the fiery plane crash, the physical and psychological pain. A conspiracy of silence.

During the "just fine" years, in 2003 and again in 2004, Cheryl's record shows arrests for "Conversion: failure to return leased equipment." I have no idea what this even means. What I do know is that Cheryl was not around when my father was dying in 2004. She stayed away from the family when she was using.

Cheryl had several traffic tickets the year after her mother died, and I wonder if she was distracted or high as she ran red lights. I feel a tingling at the back of my neck as my mind still twists to give her an excuse. In any case, driving with a revoked license was surely done with full knowledge. By 2013, she had a Grand Theft charge. She was still in Florida at the time, before she fled to Ohio and James— the "love of her life"—who was *not* there in the park with her when her heart stopped, but who did get her to a hospital and held her hand as she passed from this world.

"We haven't done drugs for a very long time," he lied to me when she died. Junky talk.

MY WHITE FLAG

**It is one of the triumphs of the human that
he can know a thing and still not believe it.**

— JOHN STEINBECK
East of Eden

A WHITE FLAG CONJURES IMAGES OF SURRENDER IN WAR. Or it may be to a higher power, or our own demons. We give up, or give in, or find peace, and sometimes grace.

Surrender can be complex for someone who is hiding from a hard truth. An abused child may unconsciously build a false identity, a façade to hide behind, always secretly wanting to be found. The only way to be found is to surrender the hiding place, but attempts at surrender may take the form of self-destructive behavior, to destroy her false self. She may repeat the very same abusive, destructive behavior of the past. Victims of sexual abuse may seek out the same experience over and over again, either with an abusive partner or as a sex worker. Or surrender may be sought through substances like drugs and alcohol.

Does all this explain why Cheryl relapsed? Why she couldn't rebuild her life? Others have succeeded in doing it. The list of celebrities who have recovered is long, including Eric Clapton, Russell Brand, Pink, Angelina Jolie, Richard Tyler, Samuel Jackson—and more. Of course, they had enormous resources to ease the way. I try to be happy for them. To take it as a hopeful sign for others that Robert Downy Jr. is now clean and sober and successful. But on another level, it makes me even more sad and angry. It dawns on me that my anger is new. Anger at her for not beating her addiction, anger at myself for letting it happen. Anger at my parents and sister for perpetuating our cocoon of evasion.

Part of William S. Burroughs' prologue to *Junky* comes back to me: *You become a narcotics addict because you do not have strong motivations in any other direction. Junk wins by default.*

The idea that Cheryl had nothing else in her life to rival drugs confounds me. When did the smart, funny bookworm I knew as a little girl lose the ability to find joy and meaning in her life without substance use?

There are also plenty of stories of well-known addicts who didn't make it. People like Janis Joplin and John Belushi, who seemed to have plenty of "strong motivations," as Burroughs would say. Though I know that inner turmoil is often unseen.

———

I recently attended a meeting of a group called GRASP (Grief Recovery After a Substance Passing). The group is intended for parents of those who have overdosed, but they gave me permission to join.

"You've lost someone close to you, of course you can come," the gracious coordinator said.

I drive through a hard drenching rain on a chilly fall evening to the meeting. As I pull into the parking lot of the imposing colonial mansion, an older woman and a young man get out of the car next to me. She is taking the last drag of a cigarette and sighs as she stamps it out on the driveway. Neither are wearing raincoats or using an umbrella, but they don't seem to care about the rain. I decide they are mother and son when he puts his arm protectively around her shoulder. She leans her head on his chest for a brief moment before they walk on. I wait until they have made their way into the building before getting out of my car. It's avoidance on my part, pure and simple.

The grief in the room is so thick I can barely make my way to the plastic seat in the former dining room of this majestic house. In the eyes of the faces around the long table, I can read the distance they have from their losses. Those who have lost children within the last few months begin weeping the moment they step into the room. Some have grown used to the pain, but carry it visibly. I know from my mother, who lost her daughter, that they will never be free of the weight, though it may lighten over the years. If they find themselves laughing or enjoying a sunlit day, the leash of their grief can tighten and pull them back. Seeing these heartbroken parents, I have a new thought. Grateful that my sister was spared being among them in grief for her child.

I feel out of place here. Though I deeply grieve the loss of my niece, and I hurt and have unanswered, unanswerable questions, I don't want to insinuate that my loss compares to theirs. My mother would have argued it could not. In my head, she still does.

As people talk, I hear the same anguished questions as my own. Why? Why did she relapse after being clean for years? Why can so many recover, but she could not? What was different about the care she got or didn't get? What could I have done to save her?

Why couldn't I save her?

Those with the distance of some years shake their heads. "We couldn't have done anything."

"I don't have a crystal ball," one mother says, lamenting whether a different kind of recovery program may have worked for her son. "In the end, they have to do it for themselves."

Only a month after the death of her daughter, one mother is not ready to accept that answer. "So many others seem to beat it, and she tried, I know she tried, I just don't understand." This mother's head seems unsteady on her shoulders, and she finally cradles it in her arms on the table.

I leave thinking these are the words we have to tell ourselves in order to forgive our own complicity. It is surely easier to believe we could not have done anything differently to save our loved one—but is it the truth?

Recently, I struck up a conversation with a woman whom I have known for years, though we are on the periphery of each other's lives. She works in a local shop. I see her once every couple of weeks and we are amiable, if not terribly chummy. I've always liked her, though. This day, while she was ringing up my purchase, I thought I recognized a new unease and asked her how she was doing today. She brushed me off with a shrug and an "okay." But, when I asked a second time, she stopped and looked at me and began to talk. She'd wasted so much time, she said, and now she was 50 and needed to get serious about making a living. I said I didn't think she had wasted her time, but she stopped me—"Believe me, I did."

I shared with her how I felt I had started writing way too late in life, not really until I was in my fifties. Writing marketing copy for insurance companies didn't count. When I told her about writing this book about my niece's addiction and overdose, she opened up to me.

"I wasted many years being addicted," she said. She's been clean for eight years now.

"How did you do it? How did you recover?"

"I just woke up one day and said, 'I can't live like this anymore.'"

She got married only a short time into her recovery. But her husband was still using. When she realized he needed a program to help him, she found him one, and inadvertently, found herself in a program she needed too.

"It's like the movie, *It's a Wonderful Life*," I blurted out. "You jumped in to save him, and you saved yourself."

This generous woman assured me there was nothing I could have done to save Cheryl—not until she was ready. For the first time, I hear this as truth.

"But I promise you, she knew you loved her. I always knew my mom loved me, and I heard her when she told me I was not my addiction—that I was much more."

SEARCHING FOR
THE INSIDE STORY

WHEN DID CHERYL'S POSITIVE MOMENTUM this past year falter? Thinking I might find a thread to follow, I look up her Facebook page and her list of friends. I don't know any of the names but recognize a few of their background details. One girl lists Hollander as a place of employment, and I assume she must have worked there with Cheryl. A series of posts point me to others who seem to have a connection. I send five of them private messages, asking if they will talk to me.

One woman writes back, saying she knew Cheryl about a year ago, around the same time Cheryl called to tell me about her new boyfriend with the house and the pool. This woman—I'll call her Sue—wrote me a long text, though I don't know how much of any of this to take as fact:

> That boyfriend was a known sex offender named Micky who had served 10 years in the penitentiary for raping his own daughter. He brought prostitutes up there all the time.
>
> I didn't know Cheryl that well. I was with Micky for two and a half years and me and him broke up and Cheryl dated him then. At first, you know, me and her didn't talk because I was hurt. Hell, I was with him for two and a half years, but it didn't work out between him and her, and she said that me and her probably could have been friends if it hadn't been for him. But I ended up becoming friends with her anyway.
>
> I felt sorry for Cheryl. I helped her when she needed a place to stay after Micky kicked her out. He just wanted more money from her.

Then Sue writes something about Micky *sending her out to work,* which I pretended until this very moment I hadn't understood.

The women were in touch from time to time, and Sue claims she lent Cheryl money a few times. In fact, a day before Cheryl died, she lent her a twenty.

> The black people she was with drove her here to get it, and I figure that $20 went right up that black bitch's nose.
>
> I liked Cheryl, she was a pretty good girl.
>
> Micky got tired of Cheryl and made her sleep on the couch in the living room and demanded rent.

Sue says he kept a list of all the money she borrowed, or he gave her for meals. Cheryl complained to Sue this was no way to treat a girlfriend. A clue into the depth of her own self-deception?

This was about the same time Cheryl posted on Facebook:

In a bar drinking, thinking about my old friends from Florida.

I had such a misconception then about what was happening, figuring she had relapsed and lost the boyfriend who held so much hope for her future—the way she had concocted the scenario for me. I accepted this as truth with disappointment but not much scrutiny.

After Cheryl left Micky and was back with James, Sue told me James was mugged and beaten and spent two weeks in the hospital, which at least jibed with the information Cheryl gave me at the time. Shortly after James got out of the hospital, she found them both crushing up pain pills and snorting them.

If Cheryl's story were being told as fiction, the narrator would either be like Nick from *The Great Gatsby*, or Stingo from *Sophie's Choice*. Both were blinded to the truth by their own preconceived notions of reality. Like them, I had wanted desperately to believe in the illusion I'd created. I have been my own unreliable narrator for a very long time.

CHERYL'S FACEBOOK POST

Cheryl   •••
July 27, 2016 8:04PM

Can I PLEASE be 14 again?

👍 Like   ↪ Share

Five months left.

ADDICT BRAIN

MY REPTILIAN ANTENNAE ARE CONSTANTLY PITCHED to addict radar, whether I am in my small Connecticut town or other cities.

While teaching a summer writing workshop at a college in coal country, I notice an older woman—I'm not sure if she's older or younger than myself—with stringy dust-colored hair, slipshod sandals and a burlap shift dress. No purse or bag. She walks in a small circle in front of a restaurant sign advertising Steaks-Long Bottles-Music, her phone to her ear, but she's not speaking. I spot a youngish man wearing a backwards baseball cap sitting on a curb talking on a cell, taking short puffs on a cigarette, then furiously tapping out a message.

The text messages on Cheryl's cell phone play in a loop in my head.

Where u at? U comin? I got $. Is it good?

People alone on the street and on their phones are suspect, even as I realize I often qualify for this description. Tattoos and lip rings do not always mean there is an addict attached, of course. But to me, now they do. I have become a profiler. A wafer-thin young man with a patchy beard walks by with a lumpy girl in a faded tank top. Both sport shoulder tattoos, and he has an especially ominous snake curving up the side of his neck. I imagine the tattoo needles on such tender skin. The couple carries their own walking music, thunderous and dissonant, from a boom box in a net slung over the boy/man's shoulder.

These people were previously invisible to me. They inhabited a world I had avoided my entire life, as if their suffering and need would pull me in and suffocate me. I believed, self-righteously, people are responsible for where they land in their lives. If I had been more aware, more understanding of how circumstances can define a life, would I have recognized Cheryl's reality?

TRAUMA OCTOPUS

The idea is a very simple idea. And you hear it from people all the time. People say, when something cataclysmic happens to them, "I'm not the same person. I've been changed. I am not the same person that I was." And epigenetics gives us the language and the science to be able to start unpacking that.

— RACHEL YEHUDA

Professor of psychiatry and neuroscience and the director of the Traumatic Stress Studies Division at the Mount Sinai School of Medicine, and director of the Mental Health Patient Care Center at the James J. Peters VA Medical Center in New York City.

CHERYL HAD HER MOTHER'S EYES and the same pain around the edges of her smile. They shared the same moment-to-moment pursuit of fleeting happiness, because it could not be counted on to last. My father told my sister to take any bit of pleasure from any day she could, after what she had been through. Even so, she never felt worthy of love. This too, mother and daughter shared. Though the reasons may have been different, Linda and Cheryl both believed they were damaged and settled for much less than they deserved. Did I believe it of myself too—a kind of survivor's guilt at being the one spared and unharmed? Charged with the responsibility to heal my family?

I study the photos of Cheryl from birth to the day she died. Forty-two years of the growing desolation in her eyes, the tilt of the head, the set of her mouth. The silly child-smile morphing later into sardonic tight lips. Resignation planted firmly in the corners of her mouth in her final photograph in the park the day before she died. I try to pinpoint the moment of the change, which is of course impossible. When I see her now, appearing to me over and over in the face of another—on the street, in a restaurant, at a movie—it is her young, innocent self I see.

From her journal, I know her rational brain wanted to quit drugs and have a normal, healthy life. She never stopped seeking out healthcare, better places to live and possible jobs—but those searches were sidelined in the final months by the daily grind of avoiding the flu-like sickness of withdrawal. In those journal pages, I try to find the moment when she gave up. Was it when she recorded the times and address for the local needle exchange? Or when she listed the towns near me where she could look for work? Or when I quashed that possibility? Did she still have hope at her last appointment with the pain management doctor? The last prescription, for something illegible, dated just two days before she died, was left stuffed in the pages of her journal.

Animal studies show dogs trapped in cages and repeatedly given electrical shock with no way to escape will not take the opportunity to escape when the door to the cage is left open—even though they can. Or in another observation by Ian Pavlov when his laboratory was flooded in St. Petersburg in 1924 and his experimental dogs were trapped in their cages by the cold waters, even though they survived they were still terrified to move after the flood receded. Some sat shaking in their cages or lashed out at their handlers as they had never done before. The same happens with traumatized people who believe there is no escape from their ongoing pain. For women in abusive relationships. For children with no place to go. In these cases, they may give up.[12]

Traumatized children often feel no one likes them, that they are less than others. I remember feeling this way through much of my adolescence, always being afraid my friends may abandon me if I said or did the wrong thing. The feeling lingered into adulthood and is with me somewhat to this day. But I struggle to identify any real trauma in my childhood. One explanation is referred trauma, or transgenerational trauma. But I understand now how silence and denial of pain and grief in our household was its own brand of trauma. If I was affected in this way, I can only extrapolate the impact on Cheryl, along with the sexual abuse at the hands of her stepfather.

Children who experience trauma often feel there is no one to protect them, no one to turn to, no one who will listen to them. The silence, denial and invalidation become yet another trauma. They feel unsafe and untrusting of the entire adult world and may internalize the idea that they are not worthy of protection and love. Feelings of worthlessness can lead to withdrawal in the form of depression, self-harm, or even psychosis. Anything to make sense of the senseless, to adapt to the frightening world.

I imagine Cheryl as a kid, slowly making these kinds of adjustments. A therapist friend of mine reminds me: All those destructive and "sick" things we all do—you have to remember that they were adaptive and protective, and allowed that person to survive. It got them this far. So they are understandably terrified to give it up.

I so wish Linda was here to share her perspective about the abuse of her daughter. How did she discover it? What were the actual steps she took? I know now that she had her husband arrested and divorced him shortly after, though she never confided in me about the episode. Cheryl never talked to me about it. The one time I asked Cheryl's sister about it, during the time Cheryl had disappeared after her mother's death, I got very little in the way of an answer. We were sitting alone in her backyard on folding chairs. When I asked her outright if Mark had abused Cheryl, Debbie shut down our conversation quickly. "Oh, that never happened." She got up and left me there. Their biological father is the only one who directly confirmed it had happened.

In our letters while Cheryl was in prison, we danced around the topic of depression and the meds that helped, but we never touched on the abuse. I asked about therapy, about the Corrective Thinking program she was in, and we acknowledged a family heredity of depression. But she still insisted she "was handed everything on a silver platter and threw it away." Her conscious mind believed this. She believed everything was her fault, and that she ruined her perfect opportunity for a good life.

And what about the lasting effects of trauma and depression in her body? Did she adopt the helpless response of some women who have been raped? Or the self-destructive impulse Freud called the "obsession to repeat"— to re-create the traumatic experience?

As far back as 1872, Charles Darwin wrote:

Heart, guts, and brain communicate intimately via the pneumogastric nerve, the critical nerve involved in the expression and management of emotions in both humans and animals. [13]

In 2014, Bessel Van der Kolk, M.D., explains the relevance of the connection of emotions with the physical body:

As long as we register emotions primarily in our heads, we can remain pretty much in control, but feeling as if our chest is caving in or we've been punched in the gut is unbearable. We'll do anything to make these awful visceral sensations go away,

whether it is clinging desperately to another human being,
rendering ourselves insensible with drugs or alcohol or taking
a knife to the skin to replace overwhelming emotions with de-
finable sensations.[14]

Most people never connect these behaviors to past trauma without professional help, but they will seek out the means to make the pain stop in whatever way they can.

I try to imagine Cheryl as the little girl who trusted all the adults in her life, until one awful moment. Maybe her mother's new husband, who seemed to make her mother happy, was left with her and her sister while her mother went out for an evening with a friend. Her mother knew the husband tended to have a few too many beers but didn't think it was a problem. The husband puts the younger child to bed and closes the door, but lets the older girl stay up to watch a special program on TV. It's a treat for her. "Don't tell Mom, it's just between us." She cuddles up to her new stepfather, trying her best to rebuild a family like the one she remembers. When he begins to fondle her, she is confused. He is showing affection, right? Love is what we all want, in any form it shows itself. She wants to get away from him, but is paralyzed, not knowing what the right thing is to do. Will her mother be angry with her if she runs from him? Will he get angry and hit her? She has seen him angry, raising his voice and slamming doors and is a little afraid of him. Later—I don't know how long after the incident— her mother intuited, or Cheryl told her what had happened. The abuse was halted, but how long did it go on? Was it just once? That seems implausible, though I hope this is true.

Maybe her emotional memory of the abuse was not re-initiated until she was a teenager with her first sexual stirrings, which left her conflicted, her muscles tense, her stomach aching. Most probably she wouldn't identify the discomfort as anything but anxiety, the normal pain of growing up. Even so, she was relieved with the drinks her boyfriend offered that quelled something deeper. It's not a difficult scenario to envision.

Cheryl's dual struggle to get clean and to find drugs is most evident in her cell phone texts. Writing to me about job interviews and five minutes later meeting for a drug pickup. The moments blur together in a real-life illustration of the addict brain I have read about; the inability to think rationally about cause and effect, about what must be done to attain the life she truly wants.

Cheryl did things to get drugs I know she didn't want me to ever think about. It would be disingenuous to ignore the lies, the theft, the prostitution charges. I want to believe these actions were the result of addiction and had little to do with my niece's character. When she was not using, she was thoughtful and kind, sensitive and caring. I hold on to my conviction that this is who she was at her core. She was not her addiction.

It is this reconciling of a loved one's true self with the addicted self which makes it so hard for families to love and help an addict. After they steal the jewelry and the car, get arrested multiple times, serve time and cycle through rehab and recovery, it's an enormous task to stay committed to helping someone, no matter how much love is there. And love is not enough.

There are, however, many stories of long-term success which also convince me that recovery is possible. It is evident that people with a strong support system, whether family or friends, are more likely to recover. Finding the right combination of treatments at the right time is essential—the right time being only when the person with the disease of addiction truly wants to change his or her life. When they have raised their own white flag. Cheryl never did.

My white board:

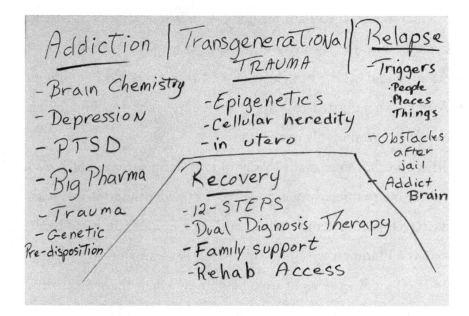

THE GIRL WITH CHERYL'S FACE

THE GIRL IN THE CAFETERIA with the black backpack and the gray tee shirt, balancing her right leg on the chair in front of her, has Cheryl's face. Not only her face, but the color, texture and length of her dark wavy hair resting just below her shoulder blades. She looks so at ease in her skin, this first year college student here for orientation week. At this young age, probably 18, she seems more comfortable with herself than Cheryl ever managed. Again and again, it is my niece's young self that I hallucinate.

I am trying not to stare too long. I'll scare her. Instead, I walk closer and feign interest in the flyers on the table near her and steal glances. It is uncanny. The spacing of her eyes, the shape of her nose, the squint when she smiles. The same. Do I think she will suddenly become my sweet niece? Lift her head and say, "Hi, Aunt Judy, I'm back for another chance." Can I bring her back if I wish hard enough?

Shaking myself out of my dream state, I look up to see the woman I am meeting to talk about her memoir work. We start toward a table, and I shift my backpack on my shoulder so I can look back once more.

I see this girl many times on this day. She is everywhere. Crossing the same street at the same time. Stopping in the Student Center to pick up literature. Getting food at the cafeteria. Some kind of tether pulls me into her orbit. I can't help the feeling that, yes, Cheryl is here, making me remember her. Making me see the girl she could have been.

TIMING THE
TIDES

I AM IN OGUNQUIT, MAINE, on a short vacation with David. The three-hour drive from Connecticut is about the right length to feel we are getting away from our Hartford suburb. I sleep through much of the drive. Why I am so very tired, I'm not sure. It may be my hectic schedule this summer with workshops and teaching, or the exhaustion of delving into Cheryl's life and death. Maybe both. Then again, sometimes I don't know how tired I am until I stop my usual frantic going and doing and trying. Like when I was working in corporate marketing, single parenting, and didn't realize my deep fatigue until I visited my parents' house and literally could not keep my eyes open. Something about having my mother cook me dinner and my father ignore me to read the latest Herman Wouk novel made me relax to the point of turning into a blob of jelly on their couch. This happened whether they still lived in my childhood home, their apartment in New Jersey, or later in their Florida condo.

The weather this summer borders on the bizarre. Cool weeks that feel like the harbinger of fall, then sweltering furnace blasts forcing me to stay in air conditioning all day. And if anyone dares quote Mark Twain again about the weather in New England, I swear I will flatten them. Today is finally what I deem to be a normal summer day—80s and sunny. When we arrive at our B&B, I immediately want to walk to the beach. The ocean is my refuge. I wind up at the beach when I don't even know I am headed there. After my father died. Then my mother. My sister. Now Cheryl. David understands, though we have never spoken about it, when I put distance between us to walk alone at the water's edge.

Together we venture out on the Marginal Way winding along the shoreline. Rocky hills rising up from the water, foam crashing against them and the sound fading as we climb higher. On a manicured lawn rising above the path is a group of bare chested, sunburned thirty-something men playing corn-hole with the intensity of a high stakes horse race. Music blares and their crystal glasses are being drained quickly of a brown liquor—I imagine bourbon. I suspect the only reason their yelling is cleansed of curses is because of the 10-year-old boy doing cartwheels nearby. Will any of them ever look back on this day and recognize its miraculous calm, their joy at being together, their health and youth? The ones struck by tragedy, I realize, certainly will.

We are rewarded at the end of the walk with the spectacular ocean views in Perkins Cove. I feel the same calm I remember when my mother took me to the beach to quell her own turmoil and have a fleeting thought this is why I crave salt so desperately. That my natural home is the sea.

At the restaurant overlooking the ocean, the menu states the twin lobster dinner *cannot be shared!* We are appalled and lobby the waitress to allow it if we order other food as well, which turns out to be a feast neither of us can finish. But the lobster is sweet and tender, the wine and rhythmic roll of the waves a mild anesthetic. A reprieve. I realize I am happy, grateful for all I am privileged to have in my life. I reach over to squeeze David's hand. It's a sensation I need to remember, and I file it away.

Walking back to our room is tougher than I expect. My hips ache with the roller coaster hills and I stop several times to rest. By the time we get back I have nixed ice cream and the after-dinner drink, opting for a shower.

The TV in our room has some kind of satellite hookup and Roku, and I fiddle with the controls while David showers.

We've already seen the images on Facebook of the awful rally in Charlottesville today, with neo-Nazis screaming, "Jews won't replace us," and I decide to bypass the news shows, hoping it's an anomaly that will fade by tomorrow. As we now know, it did not, and became a violent melee that left one young woman and two policemen dead. Right then, it was too much for me.

I settle on a PBS special—*Chasing Heroin*. Lately, I'm watching anything about addiction.

The show begins with an explanation of how big pharma, Purdue Pharmaceuticals specifically, flooded the market with a newly approved pain killer in 1996—OxyContin. From the vantage of my prior marketing career, I see immediately how the marketing of the drug worked so well. The physician testimonials backed by scientific-looking PowerPoint slides gave veracity to their claims, now proven false, of a safe, non-addictive painkiller. It's a communications plan I might have written myself.

First, the company had the drug approved for a wide variety of ailments, much more expanded than other opioids—from arthritis to back pain and post-operative pain. They zeroed in on a distinction between OxyContin and other painkillers, alleging theirs had less than a 1% addiction risk because of a time-release feature of the drug. They even purported it did not produce any kind of buzz or high for the user. This was all a lie. Sales reps were highly incentivized with bonus money up to a quarter of million dollars a year and were instructed to tell doctors, *OxyContin has less euphoric effect and less abuse potential than short-acting opioids*. As we now know, it is one of the most highly addictive drugs ever manufactured, and its original formula made it easy for abusers to crush it to inhale or inject for a high lasting up to eight hours, which is probably the biggest reason it became such a popular street drug.

The ploy even worked on the FDA, which stated, *Delayed absorption, as provided by OxyContin tablets is believed to reduce the abuse liability of a drug.*

In what seems to be a particularly evil maneuver, Purdue then developed a database of prescribing patterns of doctors, in order to pinpoint those who prescribed the most painkillers and to target them for sales. The company's ruthless marketing of the drug that would catapult the opioid epidemic included advertising in medical journals, experimenting with radio and TV advertising and establishing reciprocal relationships with doctors. A pattern that became the present model for the entire drug industry.

Even as Purdue has been prosecuted and fined over the past ten years, the company has raked in $31 billion as of this writing on the sales of OxyContin. Kentucky, ironically for Cheryl's story, battled for over seven years with Purdue Pharma in 12 claims over allegedly misleading doctors and patients about the drug and leading to the state's horrific opioid epidemic. There are many more suits pending around the country against Purdue and other companies. Statistics are hard to keep up with, but several sources show fatal overdoses are a leading cause of death in the United States with 64,000 deaths in 2016 and 72,000 in 2017.

Here's the heart of why the flood of OxyContin led to the opioid epidemic. Because there was so much of it around and it was so easily prescribed, it trickled down from pharmacies to hospitals and became the street drug of choice sold by dealers at a premium—sometimes as much as $100 for a single 80 mg tablet. From 1999 to 2010, the sale of prescription painkillers to pharmacies and doctors' offices quadrupled. And, in that time, overdose deaths from prescription painkillers also quadrupled to almost 17,000.

Even as OxyContin abuse waned with new regulations and the understanding by doctors of the abuse risks, heroin use saw a marked rise. The source of a high for addicts often depends on availability and price. My niece was part of this wave all along, probably as early as the 1996 introduction of the drug, when she was 22.

But statistics are just numbers until a loved one dies.

The story on the PBS special that resonates most for me is of a twenty-year-old girl whose parents claim she had the "happiest of childhoods." When she hit adolescence, she was diagnosed with ADHD and depression. There is no mention of how those conditions were treated, or if they were. She began self-medicating, her parents say.

A scientist on the show explains that the younger a person is when she begins using drugs, the harder it is to quit. This is especially true of opioids because of changes in the brain that inhibit the mechanism for control. This information agrees with my other research about brain chemical imbalances and the effect of drugs on such imbalances. The expert compares it to the brakes of a car being disengaged: "You may want to stop, but you have no brakes."

How terrifying for Cheryl to be in that car, careening down a mountain toward a cliff, pumping at the ineffective brakes. At some point, she stopped trying to use the brakes and gave in to the momentum of fate. Like the trapped dogs suddenly given an open door, she couldn't see a way out—to recovery—even when it was presented to her. The program at The Healing Place, counselors at the Salvation Army and Jewish Family Services. Declining the option to come to me when she first got out of jail.

The girl in the PBS story is caught using heroin in a friend's bathroom when she is 17. Her parents send her to the "best rehab we could find" for 90 days. "We were afraid it wasn't enough time," they remember. It wasn't. The documentary follows the family through two subsequent relapses, and then to a hopeful recovery period when the girl seems to have an epiphany that she wants to change her life. She graduates high school and makes a tearful speech at the graduation ceremony saying, "My beautiful family over there—I'm so sorry for all the crap I put you through."

A month later her mother finds her dead in their bathroom, with a needle in her arm and her works in the sink.

"It must have happened so fast," her mother says to the camera. I am taken by the fact that the mother's eye shadow perfectly matches her sweater.

In another segment, a boy is picked up on the street, unconscious from an overdose, and loaded into an ambulance. My brain photoshops Cheryl's face onto the scene—as close I can get to being with her when she was found in Cherokee Park. But this boy is luckier and wakes up when they inject him with Narcan (naloxone). Why, oh why, didn't they give that antidote to Cheryl?!

Early in the taped show it is evident it was filmed in 2015, during the Obama administration. Studies at that time confirmed incarceration for drug addiction is not effective in reducing the number of addicts or overdoses or recidivism. The documentary focuses on police departments around the country that are experimenting with new ways to approach the epidemic. They are partnering with social workers to implement programs stressing treatment and access to resources for recovery. Even when addicts aren't ready to quit, new maintenance programs using drugs like methadone and buprenorphine try to keep them safe and alive until they are ready, instead of putting them in jail. It seems both hopeful and hopeless, a Sisyphean endeavor. But more humane. Legislation then followed suit, loosening up the mandatory sentences for drug offenses.

This was only two years ago, but now seems like a mirage under Trump. Amid overwhelming contrary evidence of effectiveness, Trump announces, "Strong law enforcement is absolutely vital to having a drug-free society." His idea for prevention is to "tell them that drugs are no good, really really bad." As if the past *Just Say No* campaign put a dent in drug abuse. It did not. This, in the face of results from his own appointed commission to study the epidemic, which concluded treatment, and not enforcement, is called for to end an "opioid epidemic that is unparalleled." Easier access to naloxone can prevent death from opioid overdosing, but the administration fails to do the one thing that would enable naloxone to be available without a prescription—declare the opioid epidemic a national health crisis.

The night before leaving Ogunquit, we go to a well-known restaurant famed with sing-alongs at its piano bar. It's a combination gay bar and tourist bar, which is interesting on so many levels. The spirit here is rowdy and free, and I can't help thinking of Berlin before World War II. Of the Nazis drowning out Joel Grey in *Cabaret*. And now the racists chanting "blood and soil" in Charlottesville. We stay for a long time in the bar, and I sing *Sweet Caroline* at the top of my lungs until I am hoarse.

The next day before leaving for home, we walk to the beach for a last look at how the tide transforms it in six-hour intervals, creating tide pools where kids scoop up clams, and chasing tourists back from the encroaching surf. We see how the newbies to this beach have perched their chairs up to the water's edge only to scurry back quickly toward the boardwalk when their blankets are quickly swamped by the waves.

We are easily blindsided when we don't see the trajectory of our own story.

WHY WRITE THIS?

WHY AM I WRITING THIS BOOK? At times it seems like an obsession. An addiction in its own right.

Like Joan Didion, *I write entirely to find out what I'm thinking, what I'm looking at, what I see and what it means. What I want and what I fear.*

Right now, I'm trying to understand the reason one person can drink occasionally, while another says if she takes the first drink she will be closing up the bar. Why one person can try cocaine once and never do it again. Or even snort a hit of heroin and not go back for more. Addicts and alcoholics say those are the lucky ones. But I want to know, as the old song says, "What's luck got to do with it?"

Not much, as it turns out. It seems this particular brand of luck is composed of brain chemistry, genetic predisposition, and the existence or lack of trauma—to name a few pieces of the complex puzzle of addiction. Something fuels my need to unearth the components of Cheryl's addiction. That her very birth was deemed a miracle, from my sister who was her own miracle of survival, intensifies this need. Maybe Cheryl felt the burden of being the salvation of the family. We had this in common. Maybe it was much too much for her.

She died at 42, but it's the little girl I can't get out of my head. The little girl who was quick to giggle, who found solace in books, who held tight to her younger sister's hand. Why didn't that little girl have the chance at happiness we wanted for her? Why was she the one susceptible to the pull of substance abuse?

I read book after book written by recovered addicts, and a few from parents with addicted kids—some who made it, some who did not. The stories are so similar, but I remember to consider each narrator and his or her individual truth. The ones written by the addicts all have the usual arc of descending into the abyss, the awakening epiphany, the rehab and recovery. The details may change, but it is the same plot. Sometimes they write about relapse, sometimes not. But statistics say most do relapse at one time or another after rehab, and sadly that's when many overdose, since their resistance to the drug is less than they remember. So, a misstep becomes a funeral.

It seems like luck to find the right recovery program. The right mix of 12-Steps, psychology and pharmacology. Or maybe, as one friend suggests, it's simply grace.

Even if you have the resources, good rehabs are hard to find. There are many so-called rehabs without trained physicians and psychiatrists or psychologists. Many are run exclusively by ex-addicts who create convincing ad campaigns and charge exorbitant rates. As I write this, there is no legal requirement for rehabs to be accredited. There are, however, physicians who are accredited addiction specialists, Board Certified in Addiction Medicine. New York has a substance abuse counselor certification called Credentialed Alcoholism and Substance Abuse Counselor (CASAC) with training, education and a code of ethics. Facilities with these types of specialists are the ones to seek out.

The few parents who write books after their child dies of an overdose are mostly trying to work through these same questions. To be absolved of guilt. For not saving their child. There is some comfort in understanding the complexity of this disease, and the knowledge the addict has to be a willing participant in recovery. Cheryl was not ready yet. My sorrow is I couldn't keep her alive until she was ready to get help.

As long as I keep writing, she isn't fully dead. While I'm engaged in trying to make sense of what happened, it is a measure of control—another illusion I am allowing. I don't have to fully say goodbye, or dwell on my failing and losing her. And missing her.

I miss her.

Even as I write this, I regret not taking her into my house toward the end, when she finally asked, and keeping her here until she felt ready. It was fear, and the warnings of friends, that prevented me. And now I have to face that she may never have been ready, and there was nothing I could do to bring her to that white flag.

LOUISVILLE REVISITED

I ARRIVE IN LOUISVILLE AROUND NOON, already edgy, when the Alamo guy tells me the Manager's Special I purchased to save a few bucks only has a pickup truck available. I swear he smirks as he looks at my nearly white hair and 5'2" frame. No doubt the Yankee accent doesn't help.

"That's a bait and switch," I say loudly. "My contract says economy." Lately my anger is breaking through the surface.

"Economy or larger." Another smirk.

"Not a TRUCK for Godsakes!"

I look behind me and warn the others in line. "If you booked the

Manager Special, it's a pickup truck!" No response. They are obviously too smart to have fallen for the ruse. I hate them all.

"How much more for an economy car?"

I pay the $18 extra and free the other 20 people waiting.

When I came here to visit Cheryl when she was released from jail, I was afraid of what I would find. Now, walking down the rental car aisle to my white Nissan, I feel Cheryl's presence, and I hear her voice. *Now you come? Why didn't you come when I needed you?* She is whispering directly into my heart.

It's a beautiful fall day that could pass for summer, it's so warm. This also annoys me.

The apartment I am renting is on the third floor and my notes say it is #3. But when I ask for directions from a woman in the stairwell, she asks if it's in building A, B or C. What?

"Is it 3A, B or C?" she asks again. Apparently, there are different wings of the apartment building. No one mentioned this when they gave me the address. I frantically text my friend who knows the owner of the place, who is in Japan or somewhere. *A*, he writes. Oh for fuck-sake. I feel my intestines rumble in frustration. When I find it, though, I'm relieved it is a beautiful apartment and much better than a hotel room.

I have an hour before my first appointment. I'm not sure why I am meeting with the head of the Jewish Family Services where Cheryl had only two sessions last December. I don't know what I want from them. I spend my free hour unpacking and drinking a tall glass of EmergenC© that I brought with me. At least I will be hydrated.

The lobby of the Jewish Community Center is like any medical building, with bland blank walls and sharp edges. A receptionist asks who I am here to see. Strangely, she doesn't ask my name. The director comes out and shows me into her office—like every office everywhere. A computer on a fake wood desk, low metal file cabinets, shelves filled with notebooks, and two plastic chairs. I take the one closest to her. She is a little younger than me, maybe mid-fifties, with long graying hair and black-rimmed glasses. She wants to know what she can do for me.

"I guess I just want to know how things work here. What happens when a new client—you call them clients, right? What happens in the first meetings?"

When I called initially, she didn't want to meet with me. My social worker son explained that they may be afraid of a lawsuit. Apparently, this happens. When I assured her I was not looking for any details from my niece's sessions, she scheduled the appointment. Now I have to live up to my promise, when all I really want to know is what she saw in Cheryl's eyes.

She tells me they take a full medical and psychological history first and discuss how JFS can help. "We cross reference services here, so if someone needs career help, or more in-depth counseling, we find the right fit." I stifle my urge to ask how they could not have known she was an addict. And why they didn't help her find a place to sleep the week before Christmas last year?

In the middle of our conversation, I admit I don't know why I am here, or what I am looking for. The director softens and says, "When something like this happens, sometimes we just have to do something, even if we don't find any answers."

I surprise myself by tearing up—another broken promise to my-self. This is a fact-finding mission. I want answers, when maybe there are none. I leave the office dissatisfied and angry with myself. I am a trained writer and former newspaper reporter, and I should be more professional and more prepared and better at this. Shit, shit, shit.

This past summer, I saw a new play in Williamstown, up in the peaceful hills of the Berkshires. The play begins with the story of a young man who is killed in prison. His mother visits the prison and asks the guard to show her where her son died. He complies. Then she asks him to please show her, to lie down in the position in which her son was found dead. The guard balks at the request, but when the woman touches his hand and begs him, he acquiesces and lies down on the floor with his knees pulled up to his chest, one arm under his neck and the other flung over his eyes. He quickly starts to get up, and she waves him down again with motherly authority;

she walks around him to be sure she fully sees exactly how her son lay dying, then motions for the guard to get up. She studies the spot on the floor, circling it several times, kneels slowly, and replicates the position on the ground with her own body. She lies there for a full minute until we are relieved with a blackout to end the scene. I knew then I would be taking this trip to Louisville. Maybe that play is the sole reason I have come here.

I start the following day in my rented apartment by cooking breakfast. I hate going out to breakfast alone. Yesterday I bought some eggs, some Jimmy Dean breakfast sausages and a pack of English muffins. Breakfast takes longer than planned since I don't know where anything is. Apparently, my host does not cook much. I find a frying pan, but no toaster. The oven broiler will work, I think. I fire it up. In a moment I smell something burning and open the oven to find a stack of pots and pans. I have broiled an empty roasting pan to crispy.

It's a beautiful day again. Doesn't it ever rain anymore?

Louisville is very pleasant, and even when I find myself in the wrong lane to turn onto the highway, a pleasant woman flags me ahead. I wave. Thank you so much. Why does this also piss me off?

My next stop is the Salvation Army central shelter on South Brook Street. I remember being relieved when Cheryl procured a bed there last January. At least she would have a safe, warm place to sleep and two meals a day. She didn't tell me much about the place, and I assumed it was just a stopgap for her until we could get her on her feet.

After I tell the receptionist I have an appointment with the program director, Johanna, and hand her my driver's license, she waves me around the metal detector. It takes a moment for it to dawn on me why this may be a necessary precaution, and the muscles in my neck tighten. I'm told Johanna is in a meeting and am pointed to some chairs across the room to wait. Instead, I pace and take pictures, seeing Cheryl around every corner. Imagining her nonchalant air. *I'm just visiting, I'll take a corner room, please. Biscuits with my breakfast. Extra salt on my home fries.*

I'm nervous, taking in these halls, these lockers, these bunks. Did the desperation of the place—so institutional—seep into her? Feed her depression, for which she was not taking her meds, even though she told me she was? An actual girl with an overstuffed backpack shuffles down a far hall, a defined slump in her shoulders, glancing back toward me. She is about Cheryl's size, her clothes layered, worn and mismatched, her dark hair tangled. Even as I mentally place her in a category, I realize she looks very much as Cheryl did the last time I saw her.

As I see Johanna approach with an outstretched hand, I attempt to relax my grimace into a smile. She is a strawberry blonde with an armament of curls down her back which bounce as she walks, and nearly sparkle in the streaks of light from the skylight windows. She has a ready smile and an irrefutable sincerity.

"If someone is homeless, they have a weapon," I'm told when I ask about the metal detectors. "If we take them away, we take away their power, but we can't have them upstairs." She doesn't hesitate or use euphemisms when she explains the solution is to have people store their belongings, including any weapons, or even drugs, in a large plastic bag, before entering. The bags are labeled with their bunk number, locked up for the night, and retrieved in the morning. The metal detector keeps them honest. "We don't go through their things. We can't be doing that."

I learn many facts Cheryl never told me about the place. The shelter helps people find work, housing and addiction counseling. They negotiate with local banks for second-chance bank accounts—a huge issue for people with a record—as it was for Cheryl. She served her time for crimes associated with her drug use, but the banks kept her in their high-risk database and would never forgive the forged checks. I was told this unceremoniously by several banks.

Affordable housing is a big problem, Johanna says. "If someone is making $7.25 or $7.50 an hour, they are not going to be able to afford to live on their own. It's just not possible." I mentally add this to the list of seemingly insurmountable obstacles for people with a record trying to rebuild their lives. For those working, the shelter negotiates with landlords for lower rents, and will subsidize when possible. It's not perfect, Johanna concedes. "We do what we can." It all could have helped Cheryl. Why do I persist in thinking it still can? And why didn't she take the help available here? I have to finally admit it was her choice.

Johanna's eyes light up as she tells me about the programs, like the culinary training program, to help people "who want to change."

I note the religious overtone of the place, overtly Christian, but Johanna says they keep it in the background and are open to everyone, regardless of their faith or lack thereof. "It's here if they want it."

Case managers are available for anyone who wants the help, she says. They are for the most part recently graduated social workers. Was this the appointment that kept getting postponed for Cheryl last year? I am struck that they offer much more help than the designation "shelter" implies.

People can come for a bed and meals, Johanna tells me, but after 45 days, if they don't want to find work and seek the help to change, they are told to leave. "Someone else is waiting for a chance to change their life." Would Cheryl have been ready to change her life within that 45 days?

We talk about Cheryl, but I never pull up the picture on my phone I planned to show her. I mention my guilt at being here now, but not then. "You could have come in January, and she may have been okay, and then not okay the day after you left." Johanna is being kind. People must be ready to change, she says. A phrase I've heard so often I can hardly hear it anymore. "Even if they leave us, and then come back and want our help, we are always here."

And they *were* here for her. Truly, when no one else was. I tell Johanna how grateful I am for the help they gave my niece and I make a donation.

My next appointment texts me as I am parking at the University of Louisville campus library. Tiffany is an old friend of Cheryl's from middle school in Florida who now lives in Louisville. Her car is "having a problem." Can we please meet closer to where she lives, and she will have a friend drive her? **Sure,** I text back—**just tell me where.**

We meet at a Bob Evans restaurant across the river, in Indiana. To my east coast mind, the place looks like a Friendly's. The same red upholstered booths and the counter for take-out milk shakes. I don't see anyone who may be looking for me right away, so I go to the restroom. When I come out, I see a stout woman with untamed light hair, flanked by a taller somewhat masculine woman wearing a baseball cap, talking to a waitress. When they see me, they point and begin coming at me—or that's how it feels. The shorter woman has her arms out in greeting, and I instinctively want to back up, but force myself in for a hug. The taller woman stands back and nods to me. I have the sudden feeling she is the bodyguard.

We sit and exchange greetings, and I try very hard not to stare at Tiffany's missing incisors. It doesn't stop her from smiling and being very generous and open with me. Weary. That's the word that pops into my mind. Her eyes are weary around the edges, and she can't meet my gaze for longer than a beat or two. I open my menu and the two women, both sitting across from me, exchange a glance and say they aren't really hungry.

"Oh, come on, don't make me eat alone. Have something. It's on me. Please."

Another shared look and nod and they open their menus. They chat about how great the southern fried steak is here and if they should get the fries. Yes and yes, I chime in. We each order full meals.

I ask if they mind if I record us and place my tape recorder in the middle of the table. It's the first time I've used this digital machine, and I don't really trust it, but I restrain myself from taking out my notebook and pen, worried it will constrain the talk.

"I was sitting in the library and heard someone calling me by name, in this place so far from home, and I looked up to see Cheryl," Tiffany tells me. "We talked and laughed for a long time about the good times. Those were carefree days, when we only worried about what we would wear to the roller-skating rink Friday night. It was so good to see her."

At that time, Tiffany was in the rehab program at The Healing Place, where Cheryl had been after her release from jail.

Tiffany wants to help me understand, to "find some peace," she says. She tells me what she knows about addiction and the "dark hole" she says she was in for so long. About the day she woke up in Portland, Oregon, with a group of strangers and no idea how she got there. Somehow she got herself to The Healing Place.

"I sincerely don't remember how I knew about the place, but the weird thing was my sister and mother had planned an intervention to get me there. And, before they could do it, I was already there. That still gives me chills. I asked Cheryl if she had gone through the program at The Healing Place and told her it had changed my life. She said she went through half of it, but it wasn't for her."

Drugs are in my past.

"I could see she was struggling," Tiffany tells me. "I just knew. I told her to come back in, and I could be her mentor. But James was with her, and I think that stopped her from talking. He was answering for her."

Tiffany says she now understands the pain her addiction has caused her two children, her sister, and her mother. "You should meet my family, it may help you to hear how they have coped with—me," she offers. She says tomorrow I will meet them.

Before we leave, she reaches into her purse and presents me with a bejeweled handmade butterfly with the word HOPE on its wings. She never does text me where I should come the next day to meet her family.

I wake up the next morning in the unfamiliar bed believing Cheryl has boarded a plane to Paris. In my dream, she was walking along the Champs-Élysées, freed from the real prison and the one of her making. For a moment I am relieved. She has escaped. Gone to a place I'd told her about so often, that I love. In the Neverland between sleep and waking, I greet her at the airport and take her to my house, set her up in my guest room and give her towels. Hug her to me. Introduce her to my obese orange cat. The dream ends here, because I never imagined how it would work after that.

Shaking off the dream, I'm left with the question of why I am here in Louisville now, close to a year after her death. Am I trying to find a different ending to this story? Thinking—it cannot end like this. It wasn't meant to.

The last time I was here, I spent a few days with Cheryl. She was relaxed, and I thought I recognized the old spark in her eyes. I'd taken her to as many meals as we could fit into our three days together. At my fancy-schmansy hotel—The Brown—and at the famous fried chicken place founded by Colonel Sander's wife. I told her to order as much as she could possibly eat, and she did.

One afternoon we went to a mall and played at being a carefree aunt and niece. Buying ice cream cones and looking in shops at dresses and trinkets neither of us needed, getting her a very needed warm pair of boots. She picked out a pair of earrings and we found a place to get her a haircut. I thought she should have it styled and cut shorter, but she only allowed a light trim. Even so, her hair looked so much better, and I saw it lifted her mood. I goaded her into letting me buy her a couple of outfits that I envisioned she would wear to job interviews. We even argued a little bit about what was appropriate, which reminded me of shopping with my mother many years back. We never know when we are in the midst of a moment we should savor.

What had we talked about during our last short time together? Did we talk at all about drugs? I don't think so. Or recovery? Or rehab? Or the program at The Healing Place? Why she didn't go through the whole program? Was she too nonchalant about the ease of recovery? Was I? Should I have challenged her about it? I wanted our visit to be a happy one, so maybe I was responsible for avoiding this crucial topic. She seemed so much like her old self. Joking and laughing, even though she let me know it wasn't easy adjusting to the way she was living. I was focused on logistics and the material things she needed. Somewhere to keep the money from her paycheck. A sweater for the still-cold winter. Clothes for all the imagined job interviews.

A familiar dance of avoidance of the most pressing truths. In this case, the hovering threat of relapse and the pull of Cheryl's addiction. I would give anything to go back to that day and talk about it all with her, holding back nothing.

Which book should I have sent her to open her eyes? Which book should I have read myself to find the right way to help? I believed she was okay. She told me so and seemed so confident. The old boyfriend seemed to be gone, and I chose to believe it.

I was arrogant, ignorant about addiction, and in deep denial, thinking all I had to do was show up and love her.

Tiffany had told me, "It's just a dark hole and you are all alone."

Part of my reasoning to come here was to understand more about the place Cheryl last lived. I spend a few hours in the University of Louisville library to get acquainted with the city.

Louisville has a much higher percentage of poor alongside the very affluent—that old horse money I heard about when I toured Churchill Downs. More people have a high school degree than advanced college, and more die of cardiovascular disease and diabetes than the national average. There are more manufacturing and blue-collar jobs than professional ones, though healthcare is one standout.

A friend calls Kentucky very "red"—a Trump state. Maybe there is some correlation with their trying to hang on to an illustrious past. Make Louisville Great Again. Many of the ornate and architecturally beautiful mansions are now converted to more functional use like administrative buildings. The high life is still celebrated for the entire week of the Kentucky Derby, and I remember Cheryl saying how much she loved that week in the city. Was it a chance for her to imagine a different life?

I find pictures online of the Pegasus Parade in downtown Louisville for the 2016 Derby. I study the crowds on the sidelines, enlarging the photo as big as possible, crazily looking for Cheryl.

Because drug related deaths have risen 900 percent in a decade, Kentucky expanded support for drug treatment programs in the last few years. Still, most—nearly 80 percent—of Kentucky treatment programs are for outpatients only and may only offer an hour of care a week.

An hour of care a week.

Let that sink in when you consider the daily struggle for an addict. At the time I'm writing this, there are 235 programs in the state for outpatients, and only 26 are a mix of non-residential or residential programs. Less than five percent of those seeking care enter a residential program, which are shown to be more effective, compared to 17 percent nationally.

Cheryl was lucky to get into The Healing Place, one of the better residential programs in Louisville. Many people can't get a bed there. But she left as soon as she could to rent a room with a friend. She ran from the opportunity to get help. Or to admit she needed it.

It seems everyone in Louisville is carrying Narcan, the antidote to revive overdose victims. Ambulance drivers, cops, doctors, nurses—they all have it now. Johanna at the Salvation Army told me they are all trained to use it—and they do it often at the shelter where Cheryl lived her last few weeks on this earth. But she was not there that morning. She was getting high in Cherokee Park.

———

The address where Cheryl was found, noted on the death certificate, is just inside the park. When I follow the GPS to the location, I find a dog park. It's a members-only park, gated and accessible with some kind of fob. The large and small dogs run free and play while the owners gab on the periphery or sit on benches. Outside the gate, I spot a couple of picnic tables with a full view of the canine playground. One table is particularly close to the dog enclosure. I decide this is the one where she was found—though I know it could be either. Just in case, I sit down at each table for a few minutes, to take in what may have been her last view. The same configuration of trees, angles of shade and rollicking pups. I lie down on the bench to stare at patches of sky between the trees. I look for telltale signs of blood on the benches and tables, but of course find none. It was January when she died here, and now it is October, with many intervening months of rain and snow, dewy mornings and sweltering Kentucky nights. Still, I feel her here with me as the crisp sunny day assaults me. I close my eyes. For once, I let the sadness soak through me.

In the only conversation I had with her boyfriend, James, he told me they had gone walking in the park that morning and Cheryl got tired and wanted to rest. Now I know he was not with her, from the EMS report which says he had last seen her 20 minutes before answering her text and finding her and calling 911. She was alone.

I park in the Scenic Loop in the beautiful park and walk what I imagine is the path she walked. I record a video on my phone to capture what I believe is her last stroll through these rolling hills. When had she taken the dose of the fatal drug—the heroin, or Fentanyl, or oxy? Behind one of the massive ancient trees framing the path? Or sitting openly on a decorative bench with a gold-plated memorial plaque? So early on a deserted winter morning. Did she look over a snow-covered hillside as the drug passed through her heart and lungs, flushed back through her heart to be pushed out to every organ in her body? Did she watch squirrels scrambling up a tree as the drug passed her blood brain barrier, entering the nucleus accumbens? The drug would have latched on to GABAergic neurons, blowing apart the dopamine control valve that normally prevents an overflow, allowing the hormone to spill into her bloodstream with a rush of euphoria.

Where exactly was she when she realized something was wrong? Was it when the high was leveling out and her breathing started to slow down? When she felt nauseated and almost nodded off as she walked? I imagine she sat for a moment in the gazebo at the top of the hill overlooking the wide expanse of the park, waiting for the nausea to pass and trying to catch her breath. *I'm fine now*, she may have thought, and continued along the path. She probably then felt so tired she had to sit down again by the dog park. As her oxygen level decreased, her thinking may have become muddled as she watched a black lab frolicking—thinking of her old dog in Florida. Her heart likely began having abnormal rhythms when her oxygen intake became compromised. Was that when she texted James?

Wherever her first realization happened, I believe Cheryl knew it was her last call. The feeling of her heart giving way must have been like no other sensation she'd had thus far. At this point she may have had pulmonary edema, foaming at the mouth. She may have aspirated the liquid or vomit, since the gag reflex was suppressed. Did her polycythemia condition, or the endocarditis, account for the bleeding from "all of her orifices" the ER doctor described? Lack of oxygen may have caused a seizure and the brain damage.

After James called 911, the EMS report says he performed CPR until the ambulance arrived some ten minutes later. I have no way of knowing if he had the fortitude to do CPR. Paramedics note continued CPR, but there is no mention of administering Naloxone on the scene. She was intubated in the ambulance on the way to the hospital. I can't help thinking of her mother, intubated when the tumor blocked her esophagus. Of the day Cheryl held my hand when that breathing tube became clogged, and Linda stopped breathing. I realize I am holding my breath even as I write this.

How long did she lie there alone after texting her boyfriend *It's Cheryl, pick up?* That text went out at 9:03 a.m. on January 21st. The first treatment at University of Louisville Hospital is not recorded until 11:32 a.m., and admission to the hospital not until 12:36 p.m. I didn't get a call until 10 p.m. that she was dying.

When she knew what was happening, did she call out to her mother, who was already on the other side waiting to welcome her baby?

I did not go to Al-Anon. I did not seek professional therapy. I did not fly the thousand miles to see for myself; to give her a spontaneous drug test on the spot and take her directly to rehab—as a friend later told me I should have done. I treated her like the intelligent person I knew her to be. I sent her lists. I called counselors. I did not account for the change in her brain chemistry from years of drug use, which stopped her from doing what she knew, somewhere deep inside, was necessary in order to survive. I did not help her find brakes for the car careening toward the cliff.

I did not allow her to come to live with me when she finally wanted to. Every time I considered letting her into my house, my safe haven, I felt physically ill. Friends advised against it. My husband was queasy at the notion. Something inside me screamed it was not the answer. And now, I believe it would not have been.

If I had known—admitted consciously— that my niece was still using drugs, I would have insisted on a rehab facility. I was gullible, raised on illusions. *The ATM charges.* Naive. *That life is behind me.* Thinking if I spoke to her on the phone twice each day, I would be able to tell if she was using. I refused to believe what everyone told me. *Addicts lie like it is breathing.*

Maybe I am writing this book to figure out how to forgive myself for my failure to save her.

SILENCE, MY OLD FRIEND

MY PARENTS ERECTED A BLOCKADE OF SILENCE. About the plane crash. About their grief over losing Donna. And the reality of Linda's injuries. The word handicapped was never used for Linda. I even had trouble typing the word here. Calling the crash "the accident" was another avoidance. If I ever entered a room where my parents might be talking about my sister, Donna, the conversation would stop abruptly. Linda was deemed completely normal, and so no provision was made to address the intense physical pain as well as the social issues she faced.

They were well-meaning in deciding how to treat their burned and physically challenged daughter. With a patchwork of advice from doctors and relatives, they often made up their own minds. When one doctor had Linda in leg braces for a year, my father noticed her legs getting thinner and thinner and took the braces off himself. For decades afterward, he boasted that he knew better than the doctor, and Linda's legs would have dwindled if the braces were left on longer. I have no idea if that was correct, but that was the family word on it. No one said anything when she later needed a hip replacement and knee replacements. As she got older, and I imagine it may have been suggested that Linda receive counseling, my parents held fast to the notion that she was perfectly well-adjusted. Normal, normal, normal. Now, I believe the entire family would have benefitted from some counseling. Surely, I would have.

As a child, Linda couldn't hide the episodes of cruelty from other kids, because some adult or parent was usually a witness. My parents dealt with the staring boy, the pointing girl, the shuns of six-year-olds on the playground. As her little sister, I tried to protect her too. But later, she concealed much of the hurtful behavior that adolescents are so very capable of. She wrote to me about some of those times, when we were both in our fifties, and I was writing *Replacement Child*. When she was 13 and 14, all we knew was that Linda went to parties and dances with kids from school. But she told me that at most of those parties she helped in the kitchen with the mother, especially if games like spin the bottle were introduced.

"I didn't want to see the look on a boy's face when the bottle stopped at me."

I had fully bought into the notion of her normalcy. Even when the evidence mounted, with some very questionable boyfriends in high school—too old, alcoholic, liars—my parents chalked it up to normal youthful screw-ups. Of course, no one ever talked about it openly. Our fortress was intact. Nights when Linda stayed out past her 11 p.m. curfew, I would hear my parents' muffled, anxious voices through my bedroom wall. There was yelling and slammed doors when she finally got home, some punishment and groundings—but never the conclusion that Linda was acting out to make herself feel more normal. Vying for the attentions of any boy, smoking cigarettes and staying out until 2 a.m. My parents treated her like any misbehaving teenager, but never thought she may have needed help, to understand and accept that she was worthy of love. Meanwhile, I could have joined the circus and become a trapeze artist before they noticed I was gone. There was no room for me to consider my own need for care. And did Cheryl feel this invisibility too?

No one talked about Donna. Her only presence was the memorial wall by my father's side of the bed. One large portrait, colorized by an artist, her lips and sundress painted pink, making the seven-year-old look 15. Then the smaller pictures of her as a baby, as a toddler.

My mother mentioned her once to me, just once, maybe when I was ten, with a story of how she didn't walk until she was two—"She was too fat to walk, and I think I spoiled her." I didn't understand then why she smiled, but now I realize it was a happy memory emerging from her lifelong grief. My father also mentioned Donna just once, many years later, when we were discussing his final arrangements as he neared 90—a necessary conversation I dreaded. We sat across each other on the enclosed porch of their Florida condominium, our knees nearly touching. He listened intently to my specific questions, staring at a spot on the floor between our feet.

"I want to burn like my little girl did—just cremate me." It was the first and only time I saw my father cry.

The details of the plane crash and how Donna died were a mystery to me until I began writing about our family—although my mother had saved many news clips and given them to me in a large manila envelope when I left for college. When I finally opened the envelope after she died, I found her own written account of the day of the crash in her longhand script. She must have tried writing it down at least 20 times.

Reading her account brought me face-to-face with the pain my mother endured over losing Donna. For me though, the loss of Donna as my big sister was not something I was allowed to claim, even as I lived with her ghost and my parents' grief. My father kept his distance from me, which I internalized as holding me responsible for being alive when his angel girl was not. What did I have to complain about? The lucky one. Any pain I was going through was nothing compared to the crescendo of hurt around me. A broken heart when a boy rejected me, losing a part in a play, or the betrayal of a friend—I kept these problems to myself.

The undertow of my own insignificance tugs at me still, and I can't help seeing a similarity in Cheryl's remarks: *I was given everything, and I threw it away.* For her, I wonder if this unconscious layer, invalidating her experience, was cemented by abuse and depression.

It is cruelly ironic that we could never connect over this shared emotional keystone, thwarted by the very nature of our mutual denial of our own suffering. Porcupines trying to embrace. Neither of us feeling worthy enough to claim our own suffering. Did my avoidance, my obliviousness, stop me from helping Cheryl to face this particular barrier of self-understanding? Talk about the blind leading the blind!

As adults, my sister and I kept up the dance our parents had choreographed. Our geographic distance made it easier. Not long before she died, when Linda shared some new problem with her healthcare, I sighed heavily into the phone, and she stopped short and changed the subject. And I let her.

Back when Phil sent me the box of slides, he offered to help me understand more about the divorce. Lately, I have been thinking this may be a window into understanding more about my sister, and about our dynamic, and more about Cheryl. Of course, I am afraid. Afraid the facts will tarnish the fiction I've constructed and sully my sister's memory. But frankly, it's too late for that. I can't look away any longer because I'm now more afraid of not knowing, and the effects of this silence on my living family.

After weighing the pros and cons of learning the details, I decide I finally must know. I dial Phil's number.

He starts by telling me that he loved Linda with all his heart. I'm surprised to hear him say it after all these years. I tell him I remember being so happy when they started dating, as I realized that he saw through her physical scars—that he saw *her*. He seemed to appreciate her soft, loving side and her unyielding sense of humor. We reminisce about how they met at his college dance, and how he remembered dancing with the girl in the red dress. I remind him how at family dinners he had a usual joke when someone pushed back their chair and said, "I'm full," he would reply deadpan, "I'm Phil." He laughs and says I will always be his sister-in-law.

In answer to my question about the divorce, he takes me back to when Cheryl and Debbie were just babies and they lived in a condominium complex in Lakewood, New Jersey.

"I was commuting about an hour each way to my job in northern

Jersey, to Westfield." That was the reason they looked for a house closer to his job. In the interim, he says, Linda found out she was pregnant with a third child. I'm silent as I realize that she never told me. A new, fresh hurt.

"Linda didn't want another child; the girls were small and she felt she couldn't handle it." So, not only did she keep the pregnancy from me, but she also never told me about her abortion. If she wouldn't talk to me about this, of course she wouldn't tell me if Cheryl had been pregnant. I never had all the information, and it occurs to me that it is impossible to put together a puzzle with so many missing pieces. This also reconstructs my relationship with my sister. I had told myself we were close, though I didn't confide in her either when I was in the midst of trouble.

Shortly after this episode, they moved to the new house in Succasunna. The one in the slides that housed my illusion of happiness. Apparently, Phil's illusions were also dashed. "I thought everything was fine, but then I had some urological issues."

I try not to gasp, because Phil and I have never talked about such things. He was my estranged brother-in-law whom I turned to when his daughters needed help and they'd called me instead. At my silence, he goes on.

"I went to the urologist, and that's when I found out about the affair. Linda eventually told me she had been sleeping with a neighbor in the complex in Lakewood."

"Jesus Christ!" It's an involuntary gasp. But I actually remembered this as a fact I knew first-hand from Linda at the time.

"We went to marriage counseling for a while with Linda's friend, Nancy. We tried to work it out."

Nancy was Linda's best friend and also a therapist.

"I remember my parents thought that was a very bad idea, having a friend as a counselor," I say.

"Well, that turned out to be right. It didn't help. I couldn't get past it. I wasn't strong enough."

I'm deeply moved by his self-awareness and his tone of regret.

After we hang up and I let all this information settle in my brain, I text Phil again, asking for a timeline. They moved to the new house after the affair, which Phil wasn't aware of yet? After the abortion? I am pulling together the facts, but I can't help wondering if he has all the information straight himself.

I go back to look at the pictures of them around this time. At that house. Those babies. With my parents. How much did my parents know about this episode? How could I have had such a distorted view of the truth?

With so much subterfuge through three generations stemming from the first traumatic event of the plane crash, it's likely Cheryl wasn't even aware of what battle she was in, let alone how to raise her white flag. We shared more than I knew, feeling that our own suffering was insignificant. It played out differently for us—but it may not have. I found solace in music and writing, and not so much in some early experimentation with substances, for which I am eternally grateful. Debbie is lost to me right now, and I'm sure she has been affected likewise. Maybe someday, I hope, we can talk about it all.

It makes a bit more sense now why I pulled away from my family, never considering moving to Florida to be near them. We were already so far apart.

YAHRZEIT

I'M WATCHING THE SUN SET over Long Island Sound on a ferry back home to Connecticut after a lovely lunch with friends. Orange streaks cut into the deep blue, forming what looks like a terrestrial board game, reflected in the black mirror of the water.

No one at the luncheon knew this was Cheryl's Yahrzeit, the anniversary of her death, and probably only a couple of them would know what it meant. I lit the candle for her before I left home early this morning, aware that I am the only one to do it. The flame pulled me back to the instant I knew she was gone. The call from the ER, arguing with the doctor to do something to save her. Calls to her father and sister—the DNR. The desperate wish for the chance to say goodbye.

She would like that I lit the candle for her. Cheryl had no formal Jewish education, but she felt Jewish and followed some of the traditions. I believe it was a connection, to feel a part of our family. Even during her struggling last year, she remembered the Yahrzeits of her mother and grandparents. Lighting the candle today, I whispered to her, *I hope you have found peace. I miss you. I love you.*

Beyond the smeared window of the ferry cabin, the light show quickly sinks past the horizon and leaves me in the dark, the black sky relieved only by pinpoints of red and yellow lights on the shore.

LETTER TO CHERYL

Dear Cher,

So much has happened since you left. I wish we could still talk on the phone, or write. But—you know.

I've learned a great deal more about some of the things that made your life so difficult. Actually, I have come to understand much more about the trauma running through our whole family, and the silence that magnified it. I know I need to stop blaming myself for not doing more for you. You were not ready to get help—had not raised your white flag. And I finally understand that no one can do that for another person. It may have happened if you had lived longer. Maybe we would have had the chance to break the silence in our family, talking about the past and how it shaped our lives. I wish we had known each other more fully, and I am so sorry if I made you feel you could only share certain parts of yourself with me.

You may like to know that there is more awareness now about the causes of addiction and treatments that work. And there is a cure for Hepatitis C that I believe we could have gotten for you.

Contrary to what you believed, you were not given everything. Not every chance you deserved. Whether any of the new dual diagnoses or tailored psychiatric treatments may have helped you is a mystery I won't ever be able to solve. And it may have been that you were robbed of your last chance in Cherokee Park when you were not given Narcan. I keep going over and over in my mind how I could have helped you more—but I have to stop.

I know you did not want to be an addict, and I now understand more about the chasm between your intentions and your actions. You should know that I am not angry with you.

I remember your smile, your raspy laugh, the light in your eyes when you were well, your intentions to be kind and good to those around you. I miss you every day. And your memory is a blessing to me.

You were not your addiction, or your depression, or your abuse—but a beautiful soul gone too soon. Through it all, I never stopped loving you, and I am so sorry I didn't know enough about how to help you. My dearest hope is you have found your way to the arms of your mother, whose love for you knew no bounds.

All my love,

Aunt Judy

ACKNOWLEDGMENTS

There are many people to thank for helping me get this book written and published. My husband, David Schwartzer, needs to be top of the list. He lived with my struggle to help my niece, then through my grief at her death and the three years of finding a way to put it all on paper. Without his moral support and encouragement, this book would never have been written.

My first reader, my son, Justin A. Butler, LCSW, was an enormous help to me in sorting through the myriad facets of my family's history while providing incredible, sensitive editing and insight. What a great idea to birth my own editor! I couldn't have finished this without him.

Thank you to Judy Blume for all of her support of my first book, and now this one. Two Judy's from Elizabeth, NJ! I am so happy we met with the happenstance of our books and are friends. How lucky am I?

Kaylie Jones pushed me to dive deeper into the silence and trauma within my family and provided me with invaluable editing help. Her inspiration encouraged me to persist in writing the book, believing in it and how it might help others going through similar anguish. From the time she was my teacher, and now my friend, she has made me a better writer in all ways. Not the least of which is talking me down off many ledges in the process.

There aren't words to thank Richard Russo for his help and generosity in guiding me to make this a much better book, and in insisting that it is good even when I was doubtful. He convinced me that pursuing its publishing was meaningful.

Many thanks are due to my stepson, Jared Schwartzer, Ph.D., who took a great deal of time and patience in helping my very unscientific brain understand something about brain chemistry and functioning.

Cheryl's father, Philip Winkler, was an invaluable help in obtaining medical records, photos and her last effects. He was generous with his time and gave me information I could not have known without him. We also shared our sorrow together at Cheryl's passing.

My local GRASP (Grief Recovery After a Substance Passing) chapter was welcoming when I attended their meeting, even though I was not a parent of someone lost. That meeting helped ground my research and writing, and grief. I am very appreciative. Thank you also to my friend, Tabitha Lee Sahadi, who read a first draft and was generous with allowing me to interview her. I want to acknowledge the insight given to me by "Tiffany" when we met. Also, the other Facebook friends who responded to me.

Thank you to friend, Mary Beth Riester, RN, who helped me make sense of Cheryl's medical report.

Thank you to Johanna at the Salvation Army in Louisville for speaking with me and letting me tour the last place Cheryl found a home. And to the Louisville Jewish Family Services for the help they were able to provide Cheryl.

Maureen Cavanagh, Founder and President of Magnolia New Beginnings, kindly spoke with me after Cheryl's death, offering so much emotional support. Thank you Maureen.

My Replacement Child Forum co-founders, Rita Battat and Kristina Schellinski, have been cheerleaders for my book all along, and I thank them for their support, insight, love and friendship.

Author and confidant Fran Dorf listened to my writerly misgivings through this process and made me feel it was worth it to keep going. Sadly, Fran passed away this year before the book was published. I miss her being part of this book journey, and just miss her very much.

Thank you to my workshop friends who listened to early pages, both in Indiana and Provincetown. Your encouragement and good advice was invaluable.

Mary Ellen Walsh helped me paste chapters to my walls as I tried to find a way to weave the story, encouraging me all the way.

Marianne Bell O'Connell read pages and pushed me on while we floated in the pool drinking pink wine.

Thank you to Dan Sarluca and Lauren Esposito for your encouraging and helpful comments when you read a first draft a few years ago.

So many friends have been quietly supportive of my writing, which is a gift to any writer. Thank you Dorothy Marcic, Lynne Preminger, Anne Carroll, Eileen Lieberman, Patricia Sheehy, and Ray and Denise Colburn.

My cousins, Joel D. Miller and Phyllis Miller, have been along this journey with me too, and I can't thank them enough for believing in me and convincing me to pursue publishing this book. Thank you to my cousin, David Schlesinger, for reading an early version and supporting my effort.

Finally, thank you to my sister in heaven, Linda Sue Mandel—because I felt you push me along to make Cheryl's life and death meaningful and of help to others.

END NOTES

1   Maté, Gabor, MD. *In the Realm of Hungry Ghosts: Close Encounters with Addiction.* North Atlantic Books 2008, 2009, 2010.

2   Ibid. 135-136.

3   Ibid. 137.

4   Ibid. 202.

5   Van Der Kolk, Bessel, MD. *The Body Keeps the Score: Brain, Mind, and Body in the Healing of Trauma.* Penguin Books 2015.

6   Ibid. 329.

7   M. Vythilingam et al.,"Childhood Trauma Associated with Smaller Hippocampal Volume in Women with Major Depression," *American Journal of Psychiatry* 159: 2072-80.

8   C.M. Colvis et al., "Epigenetic Mechanisms and Gene Networks in the Nervous System," *Journal of Neuroscience* 25(45) (November 9, 2005), 10379-89.

9   M.J. Meaney, "Maternal Care, Gene Expression, and the Transmission of Individual Differences in Stress Reactivity across Generations," *Annual Review of Neuroscience* 24 (2001): 1161-92.

10   R. Yehuda, et al., "Vulnerability to Posttraumatic Stress Disorder in Adult Offspring of Holocaust Survivors," *American Journal of Psychiatry* 155, no. 9 (1998): 1163-71. Also "Relationship Between Posttraumatic Stress Disorder Characteristics of Holocaust Survivors and Their Adult Offspring," *American Journal of Psychiatry* 155, no. 6 (1998): 841-43; R. Yehuda, et al., "Parental Posttraumatic Stress Disorder as a Vulnerability Factor for Low Cortisol Trait in Offspring of Holocaust Survivors," *Archives of General Psychiatry* 64, no. 9 (2007): 1040 and R. Yehuda, et al., "Maternal, Not Paternal, PTSD is Related to Increased Risk for PTSD in Offspring of Holocaust Survivors," *Journal of Psychiatric Research* 42, no. 13 (2008): 1104-11.

11   Maté, Gabor, MD. *In the Realm of Hungry Ghosts: Close Encounters with Addiction.* North Atlantic Books 2008, 2009, 2010: 205.

12   Van Der Kolk, Bessel, MD. *The Body Keeps the Score: Brain, Mind, and Body in the Healing of Trauma.* Penguin Books 2015. 29,77-78.

13   C. Darwin, *The Expression of the Emotions in Man and Animals* (London: Oxford University Press, 1998). 71-72.

14   Van Der Kolk, Bessel, MD. *The Body Keeps the Score: Brain, Mind, and Body in the Healing of Trauma.* Penguin Books 2015. 76.

BIBLIOGRAPHY

Anderson, C.M., et al., "Abnormal T2 Relaxation Time in the Cerebellar Vermis of Adults Sexually Abused in Childhood: Potential Role of the Vermis in Stress-Enhanced Risk for Drug Abuse," *Psychoneuroendocrinology* 27 (2002):231-44.)

Arias E. United States life tables, 2014. National vital statistics reports. National vital statistics reports. Hyattsville, MD:National Center for Health Statistics.

Arias E. United States life tables, 2008. National vital statistics reports; vol 61 no. 3. Hyattsville, MD: National Center for Health Statistics. 2012. http://www.cdc.gov/nchs/data/nvsr/nvsr61_03.pdf.

Brand, Russell. *Recovery: Freedom From Our Addictions*. Henry Holt and Co. 2017.

Brown, James. *The Los Angeles Diaries: A Memoir*. Counterpoint

2003, 2010.

Burroughs, William. *Junky*. Penguin 2003. First published by Ace Books, Inc. 1953, edition with forward by Allen Ginsberg published by Penguin in 1977.

Burroughs, *Naked Lunch*. Grove Press 2001. First published in 1959.

Burwell, D'Anne. *Saving Jake*. FocusUp Books 2015.

Carr, David. *The Night of the Gun*. Simon & Shuster 2009.

Carroll, Jim. *The Basketball Diaries*. Penguin 1987. First published by Tombouctou Books 1978.

Cavanagh, Maureen. *If You Love me: A Mother's Journey Through Her Daughter's Opioid Addiction*. Henry Holt and Co.

Clegg, Bill. *Portrait of an Addict as a Young Man*. Hachette Book Group, Inc. 2011.

Cocteau, Jean. *Opium*. First Nel Paperback Edition April 1972. First published in the British Commonwealth 1957. Revised edition by Peter Owen 1968.

De Quincey, Thomas. *Confessions of an English Opium Eater*. Dover 1995.

Deppe, Michael et al., "Nonlinear Responses within the Medial Prefrontal Cortex Reveal When Specific Implicit Information Influences Economic Decision Making," Journal of Neuroimaging,

15(2) (April 2005):171-82.

Essex, M.J. et al., "Maternal Stress Beginning in Infancy May Sensitize Children to Later Stress Exposure: Effects on Cortisol and Behavior," Biological Psychiatry 52(8) (October 15, 2002) 773.

Foote, Jeffrey, PhD, Wilkens, Carried, PhD, and Kosanke, Nicole, PhD, with Higgs, Stephanie. Beyond Addiction.

Fuster, Joaquin M. "The Prefrontal Cortex—and Update: Time Is of the Essence," Neuropsychiatric Institute and Brain Research Institute, University of California, Los Angeles http:// physiciansforhumanrights.org/juvenile-justice/factsheets/braindev. pdf,

Gammill, Joani. *Painkillers, Heroin and the Road to Sanity.*

Gold, M.S. and Star, J. *Eating Disorders*, chap. 27 in *Substance Abuse*, by Lowinson et al., 470.

Hari, Johann. *Chasing the Scream*. Bloomsbury, 2015.

Heilig, Markus. *The Thirteenth Step: Addiction in the Age of Brain Science*. Columbia University Press 2015.

Heron M. Deaths: Leading causes for 2014. National vital statistics reports; vol 65 no 5. Hyattsville, MD: National Center for Health Statistics. 2016. http://www.cdc.gov/nchs/data/nvsr/nvsr65/ nvsr65_05.pdf.
Hillman, Lisa. *Secret No More*. Apprentice House, Loyola University Maryland 2017.

Khaleghi, Morteza, PhD, and Khaleghi, Karen PhD. *The Anatomy of Addiction.*

Kipper, David, MD, and Whitney, Steven. *The Addiction Solution.* Rodale Books 2010.

Kochanek KD, Murphy SL, Xu JQ, Tejada-Vera B. Deaths: Final data for 2014 National vital statistics reports; vol 65 no 4. Hyattsville, MD: National Center for Health Statistics. 2016.

Kusnecov, A. and Rabin, B.S. "Stressor-Induced Alterations of Immune Function: Mechanisms and Issues," *International Archives of Allergy and Immunology* 105 (19914), 108

Macy, Beth. *Dopesick.* Little, Brown and Company 2018.

Maté, Gabor, MD. *In the Realm of Hungry Ghosts: Close Encounters with Addiction.* North Atlantic Books 2008, 2009, 2010.

Marlowe, Ann. *How to Stop Time: Heroin From A to Z.* Virago Press 2002.

Selye, Hans. *The Stress of Life*, rev.ed. (New York: McGraw-Hill, 1978), 4.

Stahl, Jerry. *Permanent Midnight, A Memoir.* Process Media. 1995, 2005.

Szalavitz, Maia. *Unbroken Brain.* Picador, Macmillan 2017.

Van Der Kolk, Bessel, MD. *The Body Keeps the Score: Brain, Mind, and Body in the Healing of Trauma*. Penguin Books 2015.

Vythilingam, M. et al. "Childhood Trauma Associated with Smaller Hippocampal Volume in Women with Major Depression," *American Journal of Psychiatry* 159:2072-80

Wang, G.J. "The Role of Dopamine in Motivation for Food in Humans: Implications for Obesity," *Expert Opinion on Therapeutic Targets* 6(5) (October 2002): 601-9.

WHO. International statistical classification of diseases and related health problems, tenth revision (ICD-10). 2008 ed. Geneva, Switzerland. 2009.

Whitaker, Robert. *Anatomy of an Epidemic*. Broadway Books 2015.

Wolynn, Mark. *It Didn't Start With You*. Penguin Books 2017.

ABOUT THE AUTHOR

Judy L. Mandel is a former reporter and marketing executive. After the death of her parents, she knew that it was time to write the story of her family; their emotional and physical survival of a devastating plane crash that killed her older sister and left the remaining sister critically burned. Her first book, *New York Times* Bestseller *Replacement Child* – a memoir, is that story.

White Flag is related to her first book, exploring the tentacles of transgenerational trauma stemming from the family tragedy—the plane crash in 1952. Within the context of her family history, Judy delved into the nature of addiction, epigenetics, trauma and brain chemistry to seek answers to the questions every loved one of someone with substance abuse disease asks: What happened, why her, what could I have done to save her?

Judy holds an MFA in Creative Writing from Stony Brook University. Her essays, articles and short stories have appeared in *Kveller.com, 34th Parallel, The Tishman Review, Connecticut LIFE, ASJA Monthly, Complete Wellbeing Magazine, Connecticut Authors and Publishers Magazine, The Southampton Review, American Writers Review* and other publications. She is co-founder of the Replacement Child Forum.

A portion of the proceeds from the sale of this book will be donated to **Magnolia New Beginnings, Inc.**, an organization dedicated to advocating for those affected by Substance Use Disorder (SUD) as well as their families and loved ones. By providing educational information and peer support, they empower families who have a loved one affected by the disease, as well as those with SUD, to make their own informed choices regarding treatment.

You can find out more, and make a donation at:

magnolianewbeginnings.org

CPSIA information can be obtained
at www.ICGtesting.com
Printed in the USA
JSHW061923160922
30644JS00005B/23